the

ice cream cone

transcending transactions
by heaping on value

STEVEN POWER

Ventura, California

Book design by Sara Patton
Manufactured in the United States of America

ISBN 0-9746562-1-6

2975 Seahorse Avenue
Ventura, CA 93001

Contents

Introduction

I t is the quest of every seller and sales organization: to rise above the status of the vendor of a commodity, where transactions are price-centric, and achieve the standing of a valued partner, a place where value, not price, takes priority and collaboration is the rule, not the exception. In effect, the goal is to have business be not about transactions but about *relationships*.

Many sellers believe that once a product or service has become a commodity in a mature market, it's impossible to transcend the transaction. True, the challenges of commoditization are daunting. When a product or service becomes a commodity, prices and margins decline even as management demands increased sales revenues. To make matters worse, in a mature market customer loyalty becomes elusive, shaking the foundations of sales organizations that rely on repeat business.

It is also every seller's and sales organization's objective to increase sales and profit margins. I know of only three ways to accomplish this:

1. Increase the volume of transactions (sell more stuff).

2. Increase the average transaction value (raise your prices).

3. Increase the frequency of repeat business from each customer (get more residual).

Many sellers resist the notion that the first option is achievable in a mature market. And many dismiss the second option, raising the price, as competitive suicide. Considering the ailing state of customer loyalty in many industries, the third option, increasing repeat business, leaves many sellers skeptical.

In *The $50 Ice Cream Cone*, I'm going to show you how any seller or sales organization can increase revenues and profits selling any product or service in any market—even if your product is a commodity, the market is mature, and the price competition is cutthroat. I will introduce and explain the principles, strategies, and tactics required to transcend transactions, meet these outrageous objectives, and move from vendor to partner.

Skeptical? Here are a few examples of organizations which have done exactly what I'm talking about.

- Ben & Jerry's sells ice cream cones for $4 while Thrifty Drug Store sells them for 85 cents.

- Starbucks sells a cup of coffee for up to $4.25, five times what McDonald's charges for the same commodity.

- Ritz Carlton sells hotel rooms for $450 per night while just across the street Hampton Inn charges $46 per night.

- Hewlett-Packard sells printers for hundreds of dollars more than Brother or Epson. Lexmark sells similar printers for still hundreds more than HP.

Consider air travel. American Airlines sells coach seats from Los Angeles to London for $325 each, business class seats for $2,560, and first class seats for $6,500. The people in first class arrive in London one-tenth of a second before the people in coach, yet they pay 20 times more! Why is that?

The answer is that for its highest paying passengers the airline has transformed flying from a commodity into a remarkable customer experience, even on the same aircraft. The focus in first class is on delivering outrageous value, not the cheapest price.

What do these organizations have in common? What do they do that every sales organization must do to rise above commodity status and increase sales and margins? They do NOT lower the price! They do NOT increase advertising spending or hire more salespeople! They add outrageous value by improving quality, adding services and options at the point of sale, and creating a mind-blowing customer experience that exceeds expectations and breeds fierce customer loyalty. They provide prompt, personal solutions to business issues, deliver expertise, and in some cases collaborate with customers to customize the product or service to fit the customer's objectives and business model.

What You Will Find in This Book

While the notion of adding value is not new, what I will offer in this book is a series of practical steps that any seller can use to:

- Add value to your product or service to transcend commodity status.

- Determine if prospects are *price-centric, value-centric,* or *premium-centric,* and target buyers who recognize and appreciate value.

- Conduct an initial sales appointment that positions you as a consultative resource with a unique process which brings value to the customer's buying experience.

- Adopt a truly consultative sales philosophy.

- Implement a "pure play consulting process" that enables you to discover the additional value for which customers will pay extra, and what business challenges need to be resolved with value-added solutions.

- Deliver a value-centric proposal that transcends price, shifting the prospect's focus to value.

- Transcend *product/price-centric* transactions and begin making *value/solution-centric* agreements, which result in increased prices and profits.

- Implement the promises made in your proposal and deliver a customer experience that exceeds expectations and builds loyalty.

- Track the effectiveness of solutions, capture best practices, and build powerful case studies and references that drive future sales strategies and enable you to capture more market share.

- Establish long-term partnerships which lead to automatic repeat business and build a moat around customers to protect your revenue base from competitive threats.

The $50 Ice Cream Cone is a book for salespeople and sales managers who seek practical new ways to increase sales. It is a resource for marketing departments that need to be inseparable from sales. It is for the entrepreneur or president who must provide the value-add philosophy, vision, and commitment and then feed them into the roots of the organization — embedding them into the corporate culture so that the "heaping on value" philosophy becomes the guiding compass for every department and person who has anything to do with the customer experience.

If your business is riding the wave of a growth market prior to your product or service becoming a commodity, this book comes at the right time for you. Growth markets and robust profit margins don't last long, as you know, before new competitors pounce on the obvious opportunity, offering lower prices and accepting lower margins. The time is now to start adding value and improving the customer experience — before customers are presented with new options that tempt them with lower prices and challenge their loyalty.

Overview of The $50 Ice Cream Cone

Chapter 1 addresses the magnitude of the decision to add exceptional value to a product or service, create an extraordinary customer experience, and resolve problems with custom solutions. The goal is to encourage management to evaluate current business models and decide what methods they will use to add value in order to transcend simple transactions and increase profit margins.

Chapter 2 presents a buyer segmentation model that categorizes buyers into either *price-centric*, *value-centric*, or *premium-centric* motivations. Knowing these characteristics will assist management in determining the ideal target prospects in the marketplace, thus clarifying where the sales organization should focus its resources.

Chapter 3 introduces insights as to how consultants approach their profession and prospective clients. The three keys to successful consulting presented here represent a fresh perspective for sellers who wish to upgrade their existing consultative sales process.

Chapter 4 provides an overview of what I call the "pure play consulting process." It provides insights on how to conduct the initial sales appointment with the goal of gaining the approval of the individual with the authority to make spending decisions to engage in the seller's consulting process.

Chapter 5 equips salespeople to implement the pure play consulting process, which consists of the following steps: analyze, design, implement, and measure-improve-manage from start to finish. By incorporating these steps into a collaborative sales process, sellers can create competitive distinction and bring value to the buyer.

Chapter 6 provides ideas, methods, and examples of how salespeople and organizations can incorporate the results they've delivered to customers into credible case studies, references, marketing collateral, and business development activities—all with the goal of generating new prospects.

In Chapter 7 I present specific ideas on how sellers can transcend the status of vendor and move towards partner standing. I offer insights on the keys to successful partnering which are proven to result in long-term relationships, repeat business, and protection from price-based competitors.

This book represents a compilation of insights, methods, and tools which have been implemented successfully by my clients as well as other forward-thinking organizations. They are proven to be contributing elements in propelling these organizations into market leadership.

PART ONE

Creating Value and Understanding Value-centric Buyers

From Commodity to Value,
From Vendor to Partner

As stated in the Introduction, adding value to a product or service with the objective of increasing transaction value and profits can work for any seller, selling any product or service, in any marketplace.

Here's a perfect example of how knowing the customer intimately helped a savvy entrepreneur zero in on the right value to add to the customer experience to increase average transaction value. It is taken from an obituary published in the spring of 2007 in the *Wall Street Journal*:

> *In the lore surrounding Southwest Airlines Co.'s beginnings as a low-fare Texas carrier, then-CEO Lamar Muse's booze giveaway stands out as the boldest stroke. The fledgling Southwest was locked in a life-and-death war in 1973 with the bigger Braniff International, which had slashed its fare to $13 on Southwest's premier route between Houston and Dallas. Knowing his target customer —mostly oil business travelers on expense accounts— Mr. Muse responded by giving Southwest passengers a choice: fly for $13, or pay the full $26 fare and take home a free bottle of Chivas Regal, Crown Royal or Jack Daniels. The campaign's instant notoriety helped secure the airline's survival and clinched Mr. Muse's reputation.*

Taking his knowledge of his customers' preferences a step further, as the obit said:

> *Mr. Muse branded Southwest, based at Love Field in Dallas, "The Love Airline," and recruited attractive young women clad in orange hot pants to give passengers peanut snacks called "love bites."*

The *Journal* continued:

> *Beyond knowing his customer's preferences, Mr. Muse knew their applications. Again, many were business travelers who had to make last-minute trips and then travel home the same day. In response he innovated the "quick turn." To maintain the frequency of flights, Southwest boarded passengers and refueled planes faster, slicing the average turnaround time from 25 minutes to 10 minutes.*

Adding value has proven effective in selling commodities such as airline seats, hotel rooms, coffee, and printers at well above market prices. Even companies that sell expensive residences, multi-million-dollar business jets, and multi-billion-dollar office developments have benefited from adding valuable services and amenities, resulting in accelerated sales cycles, increased average transaction values, and greater profits.

Ideally, the commitment to adding value at every turn (what I call "heaping on value") should occur prior to even starting a company or launching a new product or service. Organizations such as Starbucks, Ritz Carlton, and Jet Blue recognized this and built their organizations on the foundation of added value, thereby entering mature markets with a competitive edge.

For existing organizations, management must wrestle with reinventing their business models, products, and services, or even grafting on a new division that allows them to transcend commodity status. In the 1980s, Toyota introduced luxury cars into the U.S. market under the Lexus brand. These premium automobiles were launched under a separate organization with a business model and customer experience that were completely distinct from the traditional price-centric Toyota models. Lexus has enjoyed overwhelming success and is famous for creating a remarkable customer experience—from sales to service to upgrading to new sales.

The Value Pyramid

There's something about consultants and pyramids. We all have model pyramids to help us explain things and mine is presented on pages 12 and 13. I call it the value pyramid. Like the pyramids in Egypt, it is a four-sided model with all sides interrelated.

I was first introduced to the value pyramid by a business consultant in the UK named Ian Hunter. Since then I have elaborated on his concept and added three related sides.

The pyramid represents how a product or service can evolve from a price-centric commodity to a value-centric offering (becoming a profit-centric solution) by adding value from the bottom to the top. On each side is an arrow pointing up the pyramid. The arrow on the left represents an increase in the transaction value (selling price). The arrow on the right represents an increase in the seller's understanding of the customer application for the product or service, how the customer prefers to conduct business, and the customer's vision for how the product or service improves their business or provides solutions to their problems (pain points) and delivers value.

On the front panel of the value pyramid, the bottom tier represents a product or service that is a commodity in a mature market. Here the emphasis on both the seller's and buyer's part is on product or service specifications and price. The selling and buying process is transactional and low-touch, and the customer experience relates directly to the price paid.

The Value Pyramid

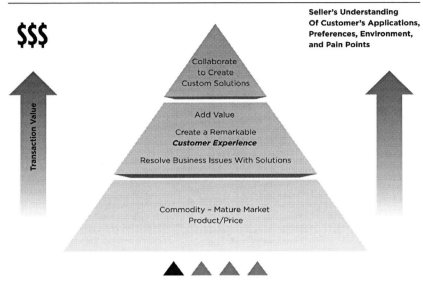

$$$

Transaction Value

Seller's Understanding Of Customer's Applications, Preferences, Environment, and Pain Points

Collaborate to Create Custom Solutions

Add Value

Create a Remarkable *Customer Experience*

Resolve Business Issues With Solutions

Commodity – Mature Market Product/Price

Seller's Behavior

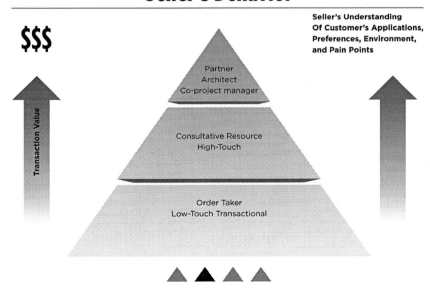

$$$

Transaction Value

Seller's Understanding Of Customer's Applications, Preferences, Environment, and Pain Points

Partner Architect Co-project manager

Consultative Resource High-Touch

Order Taker Low-Touch Transactional

Buyer's Behavior

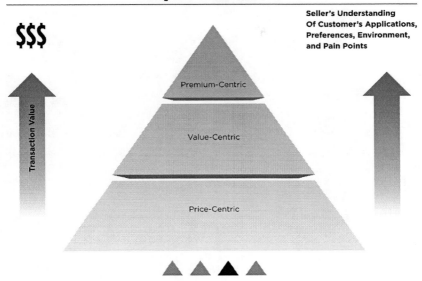

Relationship Between Seller and Buyer

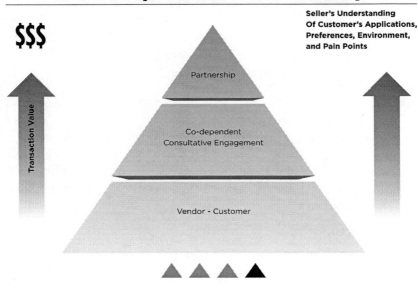

The seller may deliver the product in a box or provide the minimum service; then the customer is left on his own to sink or swim.

For example, when a large retailer sells a computer as a commodity, the customer has to set it up, install software, and configure it without assistance. On a discount airline, the customer experience may mean making your own reservation, checking yourself in, selecting your own seat, and bringing your own food and drink onboard the flight. Generally, low price equals low customer experience.

The Value Pyramid at Work

At Denny's, a cup of coffee (a commodity) costs around 80 cents. The product is mediocre, the environment is cheap, you have to add extras (cream and sugar) yourself, and there's little personal involvement from the server. The customer experience is worth 80 cents.

On the second panel of the pyramid (seller's behavior) you see the seller's process relative to the value added to the product or service. With a commodity, the sales attitude is truly *do-it-yourself*. The seller leaves it up to buyers to educate themselves on the product or service. In essence, he is an order taker implementing a very low-touch, purely transactional sales process that casts him solely as a vendor, nothing more.

On the third panel of the pyramid (buyer's behavior) you see the buyer's behavior or buying criteria. With a commodity, that criterion is simple: getting the lowest possible price.

On the fourth panel of the pyramid (relationship between seller and buyer) is the relationship status between the two. In the case of the commodity, the seller is considered a vendor and the buyer merely a customer.

Climbing to the next tier of the pyramid and increasing the average transaction value requires the seller to add value to the commodity by creating a customer experience that transcends what he would expect in buying a commodity. The seller may improve the quality of the product or service, provide financing, package related accessories or services, or add quantity (such as more legroom in coach). Business hotels offer added amenities to hotel rooms like access to a concierge lounge. Property managers often include security, professional IT, and space planning services as added value in an office building lease.

Here's a real-world example. A *Wall Street Journal* article published in May of 2007, "Taking the Common out of Commodity," features a company called Magnatag Visible Systems that produces customized whiteboards.

> *The little-known company has thrived making highly specialized versions of an item that couldn't be less special — the erasable whiteboard. In the commoditized world of office products, this is no small feat. Basic, cheap whiteboards flood the shelves of office supply stores. There are dozens of higher-end brands aimed at the professional market and classrooms.*
>
> *So how does a tiny manufacturing shop tucked away on the shores of the Erie Canal compete amid the fray? The answer: by taking the common out of the commodity. Instead of mass-producing generic boards, Magnatag goes the opposite route, selling whiteboard systems tailored for hundreds of applications, from athletic scheduling and church groups, to hospitals and mortgage brokers. Instead of a plain white surface, Magnatag boards are printed with customized grids and graphics and come with equally specific supplies such as magnets, lettering, symbols and card holders. There are boards for advertising agencies and music instructors.*
>
> *Magnatag's founder, Wally Krapf, chafes at being dubbed a whiteboard maker. "Our products are problem-*

*solving devices—they are aspirins for people's headaches,"
he says.*

*The medication doesn't come cheap. Individual boards
range from $100 to about $1,500 while systems of multiple
boards go for $10,000 and up. To date Magnatag has
sold more than half a million boards. The goal, according
to Mr. Krapf, is "to make each board feel customized for a
particular task and raise the perceived value of the product
so people think of it as a unique item that they can't
compare anything else to."*

The article goes on to say: "To date Magnatag has spent
little on marketing other than mailing catalogs; most customers
come through word of mouth."

It's All About the Experience

This example proves again that by combining various elements
that add value to the product or service, the seller can create
a remarkable customer experience that not only increases the
selling price but helps the seller gain competitive distinction.

Another example is the "upper class" service offered by
Sir Richard Branson's Virgin Atlantic Airlines. In the *Wall Street
Journal* of July 30, 2007, Steve Ridgeway, the CEO of Virgin
Atlantic Airlines, says:

*From Virgin's founding in 1984 with a promise to be
a different kind of airline, it has grown into one of the
world's most unusual carriers. It flies only long routes and
offers more amenities than most rivals. Its "upper class"
premium cabin—a blend of first and business class—
grabs attention with innovations like in-flight manicures
and complimentary limo rides to and from airports.*

*From day one, we wanted to be known for our
innovation. It's ironic—we fly identical Boeing and Airbus*

aircraft as other carriers, and yet we do make our experience feel different. It's the culmination of the way we approach design and innovation. Fundamentally it's around the value proposition and what consumers will pay for. At the end of the day, it comes back to: What can you afford to give the customers in terms of offering the best value? Consumers recognize value.

Upper class customers enjoy meals when they want to eat (not when it's most convenient for the airline to serve them), an open bar with social seating, massage therapists, and seats that recline into a private bed. Upper class seats sell for five times the price of a coach seat on the same aircraft just ten feet away in distance, but a world apart in value. Still not convinced?

At Starbucks a cup of coffee (most definitely a commodity) can cost $4.25, five times the Denny's price. The difference? Starbucks delivers a higher quality product, with dozens of possible options that can be custom-tailored for each customer. The environment is hip, the music soothing. Starbucks doesn't have coffee servers; they have *baristas*. The cups are made of eco-friendly recycled paper. And while they're waiting a few minutes for a custom-prepared cup of latté or mocha, customers are reminded by huge wall murals that Starbucks is improving the life of some coffee grower in Kenya as part of its Fair Trade coffee program. Plus, with the Starbucks logo on the cup, the customer can then walk around the office with a touch of chic caché and the suggestion that he or she is doing well enough to afford a $4 cup of java.

Another critical issue in crafting a remarkable customer experience is anticipating the challenges a customer might face and offering preemptive solutions. By adding value to a product or service that helps customers solve problems or improve their situation, you create an opportunity to transcend commodity status.

Hewlett-Packard offers its corporate printer customers Web-Jet Admin, a printer fleet management software program that helps IT departments proactively manage multiple devices and control supply replenishment and service. American Express sends customers quarterly reports that help them streamline their recordkeeping and expense account management, and adds an extra scoop of value by including fraud protection, travel planning, and even concierge services with their card. Some people pay as much as $350 a year for this credit card, and still American Express has a huge, loyal membership base, even though hundreds of competitors offer credit cards for free. U.S. Bank's Office Equipment Financing Division offers technology resellers full backroom services, allowing them to manage thousands of customers without making huge investments in IT or internal personnel. In an intensely competitive industry, U.S. Bank has the most expensive lease rates and yet enjoys the #1 position in the marketplace.

Clearly, something is allowing these companies to charge more and still have customers beating a path to their doors. That something is heaping on value in a way that makes customers perceive these sellers as more than dealers in a commodity.

Adding Value at Every Stage

The seller's sales process appears on the seller's behavior panel of the pyramid. As more value is added to the product or service and the price rises, the seller must transcend the transactional, low-touch sales process and elevate to a value-centric, high-touch sales process.

At the heart of that process, a seller must implement a discovery step to find out what kind of value his customer seeks. Again, this discovery process equips the seller to fully understand the customer's applications, preferences for doing business, and what issues need to be solved.

At this level of sales engagement, the seller also becomes an educator, teaching the buyer about the product or service as well as the areas of added value. Here the seller must become a consultant, liaison, problem-solver, and customer advocate.

At the second tier of the pyramid on the buyer's behavior panel you will see the buyer's decision criteria transcends the transactional level and elevates to the value-centric level. Value-centric buyers understand that *you get what you pay for*. They want and expect more than a low price, do-it-yourself, low-touch experience. They want and expect you to understand their needs, solve their problems, and create a mutually beneficial relationship.

At the second level of the pyramid on the relationship panel, both the buyer and seller are dependent upon one another. With a higher touch sales process, there is a natural tendency and opportunity to develop a trusting relationship, open communication, and mutual respect.

Climbing to the Top

The upper tier of the value pyramid is the Holy Grail for maximizing profits. When the seller collaborates with the buyer and innovates custom solutions, the result is the ultimate customer experience. Here, the product or service is the foundation and the seller builds onto that foundation added value, collaborating with the buyer to tailor every aspect of product or service design specifications, packaging, delivery, and implementation to suit the customer's specific needs and environment.

On the top tier of the sales behavior panel you will see partner, architect, and co–project manager. At this stage the sales process becomes a large part of the customer experience. Not only has the seller become a consultative resource, but the seller approaches each customer like an architect approaches a new home design versus a remodel. There is less focus on off-the-shelf solutions and more focus on innovative new methods and solutions. Here, the seller transcends the status of vendor to partner.

Partnering frees customers to focus on their core businesses. Selling partners must be committed to flexibility in their business models to provide this level of customer service. Many organizations are not set up to behave and execute in this manner, but those which are enjoy an enormous competitive advantage and the opportunity to create long-term, highly profitable relationships.

On the top tier of the buyer's behavior panel, the buyer is premium-centric. Premium-centric buyers realize that when selling partners are providing innovative products or services and customizing the implementation and service, they will pay a premium price. They accept this as part of receiving this extraordinary level of value.

In partnerships, sellers and buyers collaborate, innovate, flex, and team together to implement customized solutions that deliver desired results for each: customized solutions for buyers and the highest transaction value for sellers. Both parties enjoy maximum value.

The $5 Cup of Coffee

I live in a small beach town near Santa Barbara, California, and many locals don't go to Denny's or Starbucks for coffee. We do business with merchants who live in our neighborhoods. The coffee shop I frequent is owned and operated by a local couple who are committed to customer loyalty. Since I am a regular customer, the owners have learned to anticipate my preferences, applications, buying behavior, and even my favorite table — all of which are part of my personal coffee moment (customer experience) each morning.

When I walk in the shop, the barista prepares my coffee latté, and the server grabs my favorite newspaper from the news rack, puts it on my favorite table, then leaves me alone to have my personal coffee experience. Each month there is an envelope on the table which reminds me that I need to settle the bill. I take the bill home, add a 20% gratuity, and send a check. How much do I pay for a cup of coffee? I have no idea and that's the point — but with the coffee, newspaper, and gratuity all bundled in, I suspect it's around $5. That's almost seven times what the same commodity sells for at Denny's!

I have cited this example of heaping on value in over 500 speeches I've delivered worldwide. Each time, someone in the audience comes up to me and offers their own experience of how some business owner created outrageous value-add to increase their prices and profits.

A few years back, when I had finished delivering this speech in Amsterdam, a man approached me and told me how hot it gets there in the summer and how the Dutch often enjoy an afternoon ice cream to cool down. He told me of a club in the city center that was charging $50 for a single ice cream cone. I couldn't believe this until he told me the kicker: the ice cream just happens to be served by a gorgeous exotic dancer who performs in a private setting while the customer enjoys his ice cream cone. Now that's outrageous value for some, but for sure it's the most expensive ice cream cone in the world!

Buyer Segmentation, Behaviors, and Motivations

While I've always been skeptical about categorizing buy-ers into psychological and behavioral models, through experience and research I do believe that most buyers demonstrate characteristics which can be used to predict with high accuracy whether they will be price-centric, value-centric, or premium-centric.

1. *Price-centric:* The buyer is shopping on price alone and doesn't care about a value-added experience. (Flies Southwest.)

2. *Value-centric:* Buyer appreciates areas of added value such as service or customization, and will pay for them. (Flies Virgin.)

3. *Premium-centric:* Buyer expects a remarkable customer experience packed with value-added service. Cost is no object. (Flies Virgin upper class.)

From a strategic point of view, it is critical to first decide which type of buyer represents your *ideal prospect* and then design a sales process to match that buyer's behavior and motivations. There are five key telltales that will help you determine if you are in front of a price-, value-, or premium-centric buyer:

1. How dependent the buyer's business model is on your product or service.

2. The buyer's current buying behavior with similar products or services.

3. Current economic conditions, internal and external.

4. Questions asked and confrontational statements made by the buyer.

5. The individual buyer's goals and the corporate goals.

Price-Centric Buyers

Every organization is dependent on products or services that enable it to operate. Some are essential, some are nice to have, some are necessary evils, and some are luxuries. Obviously, if the product or service is not mission-critical, it does not warrant paying a premium. If the product is viewed as a commodity, the buyer's motivation is to obtain it at the lowest possible price. A manufacturing plant that prints documents which are only used internally will buy cheap printers, paper, and toner. An Internet retailer whose customers never visit its facility might choose to operate from a low-priced industrial park or even a garage. An employer requiring low-skilled labor might not pay for employee benefits or insurance. In general, the lower the dependence on the product or service, the lower the perceived value, thus the lower the price paid.

Every organization or buyer demonstrates a general buying philosophy and behavior. It is revealed in their historical buying decisions in similar products or services with similar importance. You can discern price-centric buying behavior by observing the results of purchasing decisions at the prospect's business. Look at telephone technology, computer systems, office furnishings, printers, security systems, even the artwork on the walls. If everything is the lowest priced possible option, you are likely dealing with a buyer who is price-centric.

Economic conditions, both internal and external, weigh heavily on a buyer in terms of how much emphasis is placed on price. Examples of internal economic conditions influencing price-centric behavior are organizations that operate on razor-thin profit margins such as the grocery business. This is especially true in organizations that are the low price leader in a low-margin industry. No one believes that Southwest Airlines would pay a premium for higher quality peanuts or fancier uniforms for flight attendants.

Other internal factors which can influence price-centric behavior are a temporary cash shortage, a couple of back-to-back poor sales and profit quarters, or perhaps the organization is shaping itself up for a sale in which case cutting costs to improve profits is essential in the short term.

External influences which may create price-centric buying behavior include spikes in costs of goods or services essential to operating the organization (i.e., the cost of fuel for an airline). If raw material prices rise in the manufacturing sector, companies look at all lower-dependency products and services with the intent of securing them at a lower cost in order to offset the increased cost in higher-dependency items.

Price-Centric Questions

Buyers, whether professionally trained or not, ask questions that reveal behaviors and motivations. Price-centric buyers ask questions early in the buying process such as:

- How much does it cost?

- How can I get a better price?

- Is that the best you can do?

- Why is your price is so high?

■ What type of payment terms can we get?

Buyers often make confrontational statements that reveal price-centric motivations:

■ You're 15% higher than your competitor.

■ I have to send this out for RFP.

■ Our current vendor is offering a much better price on this commodity.

■ You're in a very competitive market!

Finally, every buyer has personal motivations and every organization has corporate goals that need to be met. Some buyers want to make a statement to upper management that they are tough negotiators, or they want to be recognized for helping save the company money. Others may be inexperienced, with limited knowledge of the reality that you get what you pay for. Some may be acting alone with little accountability or input from upper management. Still others are professionally trained with years of experience in procurement responsibilities. At the end of this chapter I will provide a comprehensive table revealing the individual motivations of buyers according to title, including chief financial officer, chief operating officer, procurement manager, and key department manager.

Every organization has corporate goals — short-, medium-, and long-term—that influence whether they are price-centric at the moment or price-centric by nature. The organization may be in a short-term cash crunch or sales downturn and need to cut costs across the board immediately. On the other hand, it may be a market leader in a growth market looking for the best return on investment.

Price-centric individuals who are motivated to make a statement to their bosses, or who are accountable for getting the lowest price, will:

- Get as much information from as many potential vendors as possible.

- Validate they are getting the lowest price via RFP or bid.

- Share little information with sellers regarding current costs or the seller's competitive status.

- Share current cost information that may not be trustworthy.

- Not provide sellers access to top-level decision makers or higher level influencers.

- Negotiate early and often on price, terms, delivery, and contract inclusions.

- Ask sellers to itemize each component of pricing as line items.

Generally, price-centric organizations with price-centric corporate goals will:

- Have professionally trained purchasing management and departments with documented procurement protocols.

- Have a tendency to RFP or bid almost all procurements.

- Usually be in a very competitive industry and operate on low profit margins.

- Have multiple divisions, locations, and subsidiaries that benefit from standardization and competitive procurement practices.

- Be publicly held and accountable to shareholders, or be a government contractor accountable for complying with government regulations requiring competitive procurement practices.

- Have three or more competing vendors for the same or similar products or services.

Then there's the family-owned and -operated business, an organization often misread by sellers. An entrepreneur may not have a formal purchasing department, procurement officers, multiple divisions, or shareholders, but what they do have is a social system, some with two to three generations of family to support! In this case you may experience even more intense price-centric behavior, since every dollar saved goes into the coffers of the family social system.

Value-Centric Buyers

As an organization's dependency on a product or service increases, the perceived value of the product or service increases. Instead of focusing on price, value-centric buyers have a wider view of the importance of quality, reliability, warranties and guarantees, support resources, and the vendor's track record.

Value-centric buyers are more likely to require some customization in the design of the product or service offering. Often, value-centric buyers prefer to get their fingerprints on the implementation of the product or service within their organization after the sale.

Value-centric buyers tend to be collaborative and consider sellers to be more like partners, not merely vendors. They know that you need to be profitable and inspired in order to deliver on your promises. If they treat you like an order taker, you'll do the minimum, nothing more. In fact, many buyers become value-centric after two or three bad experiences as a price-centric buyer. Perhaps they have experienced the often disastrous results of accepting the lowest bid.

Like price-centric buyers, value-centric buyers demonstrate their buying philosophy in current buying behavior of similar products and services with similar importance. They may not buy top-of-the-line computers, printers, or furniture, but they're not buying bargain basement products either. They may not be located in the city center high rise (premium), but they are in a respectable business district (value), not 30 miles out in the warehouse district (price).

Most promising for you, value-centric buyers will demonstrate a desire for a win/win outcome, share trustworthy information on current costs, and instead of going to bid or RFP, may limit the evaluation of vendors to the top three market leaders—not even inviting the low-price market leader to the discussion.

Internal economic conditions influencing value-centric buyers include: the buyer is operating at reasonable profit margins, the cash position is stable, the organization is not posturing for a sale, and short-, medium-, and long-term sales revenue targets are attainable. Externally, perhaps their market is not yet mature and there are no external factors squeezing them to cut costs.

The economic situation that sellers dream about is when the buyer has decided to add value to their own products either to increase profits or to create a competitive advantage. This creates incredible opportunities for you to offer value-added solutions that help them achieve their goals.

Value-Centric Questions

Value-centric buyers will ask questions that are very different from price-centric buyers. These questions will focus on:

- Quality control programs incorporated into manufacturing.
- Reliability ratings from independent research services.
- Ongoing support programs.

- References with substantial tenure using the product or service in a similar environment.

- Gaining access to the seller's mid- and top-level management before and after the sale.

- The exact nature and agenda for conducting account reviews.

- Specifics on program administration.

In other words, the value-centric buyer wants long-term reliability as well as a relationship with the seller who delivers added value.

With value-centric prospects, the buyer's personal goals are generally aligned with the corporate goals. The outcome is to develop a mutually dependent relationship with a reliable resource that transcends vendor status. The individual buyer views the selling organization as a consultative resource, and understands that by limiting the evaluation process to the top three value partner candidates they will receive the best education. They also recognize that selecting one of the top three resources in the market means a lower risk of making a mistake and personally having to answer for a poor decision on an under-performing vendor.

In the value-centric organization, management often likes to get its fingerprints on the entire process, from the proposal to the crafting of contracts to implementation and ongoing project management. Often the value-centric prospect's upper management wants to participate in the process to assure internal ownership and minimize the risk associated with turning the entire implementation over to a vendor.

Premium-Centric Buyers

At the top of the buying behavior pyramid is the Holy Grail, the premium-centric buyer. Premium-centric buyers are totally dependent on a product or service. Examples include the $30 million GulfStream jet for an executive jet service, the $20 million clean room for a computer chip manufacturer, and the $100-per-square-foot retail space for a Rodeo Drive boutique displaying the new Louis Vuitton Tribute Patchwork handbag that sells for $52,500. Hundreds of products and services are essential to the companies that employ them: to generate revenues and profits, create a prestigious image, or generate a traffic flow of *ideal prospects*. Without them, the companies cannot operate.

At this level, reliability and quality are so critical that the executive jet service may buy two jets and hire backup pilots to assure 100% uptime. At this level of value, the relationship with the seller and ongoing support is critical; any missteps or downtime could have a devastating financial impact or legal consequences.

Because the product or service is so critical and is at the heart of the buyer's ability to conduct business, premium buyers can be very demanding. They may want to be involved in every aspect of the transaction. At this level, such buyers often insist on being part of design, manufacturing, packaging, delivery, implementation, and support.

Here is an extreme example of how premium-centric buyers may wield more than casual influence in the design phase of a product. According to a *Wall Street Journal* article published in May of 2007:

> *In December of 2006 Apple CEO Steve Jobs met with Cingular Wireless CEO Stan Sigman. Apple and Cingular had been co-developing the iPhone for two years and were weeks away from launching the product, yet this was the first time Mr. Sigman got to see the phone. For three hours, Mr. Jobs played with the device, with its touch-screen that allows users to view contacts, dial numbers*

and flip through photos with the swipe of a finger. Mr. Sigman looked on in awe.

Behind the scenes in the making of the iPhone, Apple bucked the rules of the cell phone industry by wresting control away from the normally powerful wireless carriers. These service providers usually hold enormous sway over how phones are developed and marketed—controlling every detail. Not so with Apple and Cingular. Only three executives at Cingular got to see the iPhone before it was announced. Cingular agreed to leave its brand off the body of the phone. It also abandoned its usual insistence that the phone carry Cingular software for Web surfing, ring tones and other services.

Usually, carriers catch more than a glimpse of the products their handset partners are working on. They get to provide input on what applications or features might make the device more marketable. Not this time. Several small teams within Cingular worked on the project, but each handled its own special task without knowing what the other teams were up to. Employees had code names for the project to avoid mentioning Apple by name. Cingular sent a team of technical personnel to Apple's offices to test the device, making sure it would work on the carrier's network. That rigorous process is normal for the release of any phone. But this time, technicians weren't allowed to handle or see the actual phone. Instead, they were given access to a dummy version that would only allow them to do the necessary network test.

Another example of this extreme dependency (and therefore premium buying behavior) is Kinko's, which buys copier/printers, service agreements, and toner from Xerox, the most expensive vendor in the market. Kinko's could save a ton of money in operating costs by buying less expensive equipment from competing vendors, going out to bid in the open market for service, and buying remanufactured toner cartridges at a fraction of the cost. Why don't they? Kinko's is wholly dependent on copier/printers to satisfy customers and generate revenues. The end result of the copier/printer is prints, which reflect the quality of Kinko's. The reliability and quality output of the devices creates a reliable and predictable customer experience that keeps customers coming back. Saving money on core components that are essential in creating the customer experience makes no sense. Because of this, some organizations are not the least bit interested in saving money in certain aspects of the business. Morton's Steak House doesn't shop around to save money on choice meat. Apple doesn't spend time and resources chiseling down the price of prime Times Square signage for iPod ads.

Premium-centric buyers are often premium buyers in many elements of their business. Often they will use premium law firms, accountants, consultants, and supply chain managers— right down to the premium coffee served in the break room.

Often premium-centric buyers are this way due to internal and external economic factors. Profits may be through the roof, with hordes of cash in reserve and future earnings looking great (such as Exxon/Mobil and Google). They may be in a growth market with little competition (eBay), or perhaps they are a proven premium brand in their industry who sets the industry standard for quality, reliability, and prestige (Rolex).

Premium-Centric Questions

Premium-centric buyers ask questions that are the opposite extreme of price-centric buyers:

- To what degree can we customize the design of the product or service?

- Can we private-label the product or service?

- Will you enable us to implement the product or service internally?

- Will you allow us to audit your financials?

- Can we interview your top management team?

- Will you allow us to tour your facilities?

- Are you interested in a revenue/profit-sharing relationship?

- Who are your strategic partners and key vendors?

- Can we audit their financials, interview their top management, and tour their facilities?

The premium-centric buyer's individual goals and behaviors are consistent with the corporate goals. Generally, individual premium buyers are seasoned executives with sound judgment based on training, experience, research, and a network of resources. These individuals are generally highly collaborative internally, constantly engaging top management, key department managers, and other established partners and vendors. Once they have educated themselves, collaborated internally and externally, and come to a conclusion, often they will collaborate with only one or two possible candidates to determine who will become their new partner.

The corporate goals of premium-centric buyers include delivery of the quality, reliability, and service support promised as well as hyper-communication between the partners. They also expect flexibility, accessibility to everyone involved in implementation, and a high level of accountability.

I have presented five criteria for sellers to weigh in order to determine if a prospect is price-, value-, or premium-centric. Now I must provide a warning against adhering literally to these criteria and putting prospects into categories that may meet the assumptions and appearances presented here, yet be a hundred miles off the mark. Some prospects will appear and even behave as price-centric in some areas of the business, while in fact they are a value or even a premium buyer in other aspects of the business. It is critical to conduct a thorough assessment of each prospect's business model and determine:

1. What the prospect is highly dependent on.

2. Current buying behavior in similar products and services.

3. Current economic conditions (internal and external).

4. Questions asked and statements made by buyers.

5. The prospect's individual and corporate goals prior to categorizing buyers.

Use these five criteria with caution. Beware labeling buyers as price-centric lock, stock, and barrel—they can surprise you.

Motivations of Decision Makers and Influencers

Many business-to-business buying decisions are made and influenced by decision teams composed of managers from Finance, Operations, Purchasing, and various key departments.

Each of these team members comes to the decision making table with personal motivations and personal agendas. These conditions within the buying environment can present enormous challenges. Your goals should be to:

1. Identify which individuals with what titles influence the buying decision.

2. Seek out and develop a relationship with each decision influencer.

3. Understand each influencer's objectives, challenges, job responsibilities, and motivations.

4. Customize marketing collateral, sales presentations, demonstrations, and proposals to each audience.

Here are findings from my research on the essential job activities and top motivators of four decision domains: Finance, Operations, Purchasing, and key departmental managers.

Finance

These decision makers and influencers represent job titles including chief financial officer, vice president of finance, controller, and in some mid-sized and small organizations, the president. In large accounts this includes mid-level management titles of people within the finance department who report to top-level management.

One important factor to keep in mind when marketing or selling to top financial decision makers is that they comprehend the relationship between price and value. They understand that superior quality and reliability come with associated costs. If they view the product or service as a commodity, they will push the decision down to Purchasing. However, if they view the product or service as critical to their business or see it as an opportunity to significantly improve business processes, they are more likely to personally engage in the evaluation of such products or services.

In the financial arena, it is critical that marketers and sellers focus their communication with decision makers, emphasizing the financial benefit the product or service offers to the organization. By nature, financial decision makers are analytical and will evaluate current expenses and total cost of ownership with the goal of reducing costs, increasing productivity, or gaining greater control over expenses.

In my research, I found the top motivations in the financial domain to include:

- *Evaluating and controlling operating expenses.* Sellers providing comprehensive operating cost analysis will be viewed as bringing added value to the sales/buying process.

- *Knowing the total cost of ownership.* Beyond operating costs, elements considered in TCO include costs of administration related to vendors and contracts, human productivity, labor costs, and service and maintenance, to name a few.

- *The seller's understanding of the buyer's business issues.* Financial decision makers appreciate sellers who have a clear understanding of the buyer's business sector (vertical market), business model, and overall objectives and challenges. Sellers who display a comprehensive understanding of the buyer's business processes and present innovative solutions are regarded as competitive favorites over those who simply recommend turnkey products and services.

The following pages present buyer research findings in two areas: first, the essential activities of the job and second, title-specific motivations. The essential activities of the job include the key responsibilities of the job title and the activities the decision maker engages in on a daily basis. The motivations are personal desired outcomes of the decision makers.

Sellers should pay close attention in determining how their product or service, expertise, and resources can help decision makers effectively perform essential job activities and satisfy personal motivations.

Essential Job Activities and Motivations for Financial Decision Makers

Essential Job Activities

- Prepare timely and accurate filings of financial statements.

- Prepare timely and accurate budgets.

- Forecast sales, costs, profits.

- Compare actual results to forecast.

- Advise department heads on budget compliance and financial issues impacting budgets.

- Identify opportunities to:
  - Reorganize departments.
  - Downsize workforce.
  - Eliminate redundancy.
  - Pounce on opportunity.

- Conduct internal audits, report findings, and hold management accountable for implementing adjustments.

- Maintain successful investor relations.

- Comply with government regulations.

- Conduct cost-benefit analysis.

- Manage operating cash and capital growth.

- Analyze industry trends and assist CEO, board of directors, and senior executives in developing appropriate responses and strategies.

- Develop and implement systems to improve productivity and reduce costs, resulting in improved overall effectiveness of the enterprise.

- Evaluate potential strategic partners.

- Strengthen link between strategic objectives and operational and financial plans.

Motivations

- Maximize profits and shareholder value.

- Maximize return on investment.

- Minimize and manage risk and liability:
  - Loss (capital and property).
  - Credit.
  - Board of directors.
  - Employee safety.

- Improve cash flow.

- Convert variable costs to fixed costs.

- Streamline vendors and administration.

- Achieve measurable and sustainable results.

- Understand ongoing costs—TCO.

- Seize opportunities.

- Improve productivity.

- Reduce accounts receivable time.

- Improve inventory turns.

- Reduce waste, redundancy, and dysfunction.

- Improve employee morale and retention.

- Gain knowledge of current:
  - Costs/TCO/ROI.
  - Risk.
  - Inventory.
  - Waste, redundancy, dysfunction.
  - Productivity.

- Improve employee morale.

- Align with proactive partners, not vendors.

One must keep in mind that while financial managers are primarily focused on the bottom line, they tend to be conceptual and visionary thinkers who often view their organization *from the 40,000-foot level*. If marketing and sales organizations approach them on this level, with resources and tools which motivate them to take a closer look at the financial impact of the product or service, they will likely respond with an open invitation.

Operations

These decision influencers represent job titles including chief operating officer and, in some mid-sized accounts, facilities manager. While CFOs and VPs of finance may view the organization from a 40,000-foot view and tend to be strategic and visionary, operations management tends to view the enterprise from the ground level, focus on tactics, and have a tendency to *sweat the small stuff*.

Operations management is constantly looking for processes to improve, standardize, and scale enterprise wide. Much focus is placed on logistics and the efficiency found in streamlining processes, facilities, human labor, and communication. The emphasis is on how to make things run better — more smoothly and cost-effectively. The mantra in Operations is: "Do more with less." The nagging question is: "How can we achieve more productivity without adding more labor, equipment, technology, or financial resources?"

Operations professionals often streamline procurement and management processes by consolidating vendors via single sourcing. By sourcing products and services from a single vendor, Operations can better manage the relationship and hold vendors accountable.

Essential Job Activities and Motivations for Operations Decision Makers

Essential Job Activities

- Develop and implement systems to improve productivity and reduce costs, resulting in improved overall effectiveness of the enterprise.

- Evaluate space/facilities requirements, facilities layout, and utilization of space.

- Develop accurate budgets for investments in:
  - Space.
  - Equipment.
  - Furnishings.
  - Support personnel.
  - Security.
  - Maintenance.

- Identify opportunities to:
  - Reorganize departments.
  - Downsize workforce.
  - Eliminate redundancy.

- Comply with safety regulations.

- Create a quality work environment.

- Evaluate potential strategic partners.

- Be involved in negotiating contracts with vendors and partners.

- Improve communication and collaboration between managers.

- Analyze and compare options/alternatives.

Motivations

- Meet internal customers' expectations for value, service, quality.

- Simplify business processes.

- Streamline communication between managers, employees, and vendors.

- Keep harmony between key department managers.

- Minimize and manage risk and liability:
  - Loss (capital and property).
  - Credit.
  - Board of directors.
  - Employee safety.

- Streamline vendors and administration.

- Understand ongoing costs—TCO.

- Improve productivity.

- Reduce waste, redundancy, and dysfunction.

- Improve employee morale and retention.

- Gain knowledge of current:
  - Costs/TCO/ROI.
  - Risk.
  - Inventory.
  - Waste, redundancy, dysfunction.
  - Productivity.
  - Employee morale.

- Align with proactive partners, not vendors.

If marketing and sales organizations approach operations management from the ground-level view, using presentations and proposals that assist them in understanding the *positive logistical impact* of the product or service on the entire organization, they will be more successful.

Purchasing

These decision influencers represent job titles including chief procurement officer and purchasing director/manager. Working closely with financial management, purchasing managers often share enormous responsibility and influence in decision making. Once their financial counterparts have approved an overall strategy, it is the purchasing manager's role to evaluate, negotiate, initiate, and administer contracts with vendors.

A common motivation of purchasing managers is streamlining the number of vendors with whom they do business. When you view the purchasing process from the start through the ongoing administration, it's clear that by reducing the number of vendors, Purchasing can save tremendous time, money, and headaches.

My research revealed that in order to select one vendor, Purchasing will usually see four to six sales presentations, draft and distribute a request for proposal, research the top two to three contenders, then negotiate a final contract and implementation plan with one vendor, who will then require ongoing management in the form of contract administration and account reviews. Keep in mind that this arduous and time-consuming process applies to *every vendor* the organization uses — which for large organizations can be hundreds or even thousands. By consolidating vendors purchasing departments can save time and money — seeing fewer sales presentations, administering fewer contracts, processing fewer invoices, and conducting fewer account reviews.

Many purchasing departments have developed vendor selection criteria as part of procurement protocols. Some elements commonly included in these criteria are:

- *Financial stability.* Purchasing will want to verify the vendor's financial strength to determine if they are going to be around to provide ongoing support throughout the term of the contract.

- *Geographic support in sales, service, and administration.* Can the vendor meet the diverse needs of all locations throughout the organization's geographic scope?

- *Vendor experience (expertise) with similar clients.* Does the vendor have a track record implementing a similar scope of work in a similar environment? Or are they out of their league?

- *Vendor resources.* Does the vendor possess qualified personnel to help implement the project? Do they demonstrate depth in resources beyond the salesperson?

- *Infrastructure.* Does the vendor have the physical ability to deliver on their promises? Do they have the management team, technology (communications, manufacturing, inventory controls), quality control programs, account review process, and a disaster plan?

- *Financing.* Does the vendor offer flexibility in structuring its payment terms to fit the requirements and desires of the organization?

- *Contracts.* Does the vendor offer flexibility in its contracts?

- *Competitive pricing.* Purchasing managers must have in place a process which allows them to compare all the elements related to pricing. When evaluating competitive quotations, purchasing managers indicated that they become suspicious of quotations that fall well below the competitive group of vendors. Their reasoning was that extremely low bids often equate to low performance. A price that fails to return a profit for the vendor can affect the vendor's ability to provide support or even survive.

■ *Hidden costs.* Purchasing managers want to understand potential surprise costs upfront.

Essential Job Activities and Motivations for Purchasing Decision Makers

Essential Job Activities

■ Collaborate with internal department managers to determine specific requirements for products, services, equipment, support, etc.

■ Prepare and release requests for proposals and bid specifications.

■ Analyze and compare options/alternatives available to meet specified requirements.

■ Gain an education on all potential products, services, and vendors who may contribute to the enterprise's implementation of business model.

■ Gain intimate knowledge of vendor's:
  – Capabilities.
  – Competitive advantages.
  – Resources.
  – Products/services.

■ Evaluate, select, and negotiate with current and proposed vendors and strategic partners.

- Obtain products and services at a competitive price.

- Obtain the best possible payment terms from vendors.

- Obtain delivery or implementation of products and services when needed.

- Gain knowledge of current:
    - Operating costs/TCO.
    - Waste, redundancy, dysfunction.

- Keep current vendors competitive.

- Visit vendor facilities.

- Conduct account/performance reviews with current vendors.

- Identify ways to improve vendor performance.

Motivations

- Meet internal customers' expectations for value, service, quality.

- Obtain products and services at a competitive price.

- Obtain the best possible payment terms from vendors.

- Obtain delivery or implementation of products and services when needed.

- Simplify processes related to releasing purchase orders.

- Keep harmony between key department managers.

- Streamline the number of vendors and related administration.

- Streamline communication with vendors.

- Make informed decisions based on information that can be validated.

- Align with proactive partners, not vendors.

- Understand ongoing costs—TCO of proposed products and services.

- Reduce waste, redundancy, and dysfunction.

- Minimize risk associated with commitments made to vendors, products, and services.

- Reverse risk with warranties and guarantees.

- Appear to superiors as competent, thorough, and tough on vendors.

Since many final decisions are made in Purchasing, it would behoove sales organizations to first identify Purchasing's vendor selection criteria and then design custom programs, presentations, and proposals incorporating that criteria and the major motivations listed above in order to gain a competitive advantage.

Key Departmental Managers

Most sales processes and marketing collateral overlook the important role individual key departmental managers play in the decision process.

This grassroots decision influencer is an important contributor to the process and a valuable ally to other decision influencers. Department managers must also appease employees and manage the internal politics involved in marshaling any significant changes in the workplace.

Essential Job Activities and Motivations for Key Department Management Decision Makers

Essential Job Activities

■ Evaluate department's requirements and applications for personnel, products, equipment, services, technology, etc., and submit recommendations to meet these requirements.

■ Justify requirements and related budgets to:
  - Finance.
  - Operations.
  - Purchasing.

■ Collaborate with Purchasing to implement all new products, equipment, and services.

■ Optimize implementation of all products, equipment, programs, and services.

■ Develop and adhere to departmental budget.

■ Manage department personnel, processes, resources.

■ Identify ways to improve departmental performance.

■ Comply with directives from:
  - Human Resources.
  - Procurement.
  - Security.
  - Operations.
  - Finance.

Motivations

■ Meet internal customers' expectations for value, service, quality.

■ Simplify and streamline processes to improve department's effectiveness and productivity.

■ Keep employees happy and productive.

■ Maintain as much control as possible over processes, resources, equipment, information, etc. at a local level.

■ Reduce waste, redundancy, and dysfunction.

■ Minimize risk and exposure of mistakes.

■ Appear to superiors as competent.

■ Get things done!

■ Get promoted!

Once again, identifying each decision maker's predictable buying behavior, essential activities of the job, and personal motivations enables you to develop a relationship, speak the language, and customize marketing collateral and proposals to each audience—vastly increasing your effectiveness.

The most important mantra of any successful sales organization is "Know thy audience." The second most important is "Know how to consult thy audience," which we will cover next.

PART TWO

The Pure Play Consulting Process

CHAPTER 3

A Truly Consultative Approach to Sales

Much has been said and written about consultative selling, and many organizations and salespeople practice consultative sales behavior to various degrees. The term "consultative selling" implies that sellers approach prospective clients as a consultative resource, offering expert advice.

However, surveys of executive buyers reveal that while many sellers call themselves consultants, the consultant's hat comes off early in the process and the seller's hat goes on. Surveys also show that early in the sales process, many salespeople migrate into generic, "We, us, our products/services, our company, and our programs" presentations and self-serving questions designed to identify low-hanging sales opportunities. These traditional presentations and *qualifying* tactics commonly come across as superficial and will backfire on sellers attempting to position themselves as consultative resources. These sales techniques can also create an adversarial relationship, resulting in low trust and low communication, yielding sellers little competitive distinction as the buyer fails to perceive any true value in engaging the seller.

If you are to present yourself as an expert consultative resource, you must approach the perspective client in a truly consultative manner early on and maintain that posture while striking a balance with a collaborative sales process.

By combining a truly consultative approach with a collaborative process, you can create a *value-added buying experience* for the customer which allows you to transcend transactions and leads to increased sales and long-term customer loyalty.

A Quick Digression: The Three Keys to Successful Consulting

Sometimes in life, lessons are learned through formal education and experience; others are learned serendipitously. The traditional consulting process I present later in this section I learned via formal education and nearly 20 years in the profession. The unique approach to consulting which I will present here I learned by coincidence.

When I started my consulting business, I really wasn't sure what consultants did or how they approached their profession. In my first year of business I attended many seminars put on by big-time consultants that helped me understand the traditional consulting process, but not how I should approach the profession. Then, one night on an airplane, I met an elderly woman who was elegant and articulate. We chatted for a while and in the course of conversation she asked me what I did professionally and I responded that I was a consultant. She proceeded to share with me insights that profoundly changed the way I approach my profession and my clients. To this day her advice is at the heart of my training programs, which are designed to enable salespeople to position themselves as consultative resources and practice true consultative behavior.

This wise woman shared with me three things which consultants bring to the table that clients desperately need, value, and for which they will pay a premium: expertise, innovation, and acceleration.

Expertise

What's the first thing buyers want from sellers? The same thing you want when you go into BestBuy to look at iPods and find yourself standing in front of a giant display case containing 36 different models ranging in price from $49 to $349. You want knowledge and expertise to help you navigate an unfamiliar landscape. Knowledge helps buyers make better informed decisions and therefore feel that they are better decision makers.

There are at least three areas of knowledge (expertise) that consultants should be ready to offer prospects:

1. Knowledge of your industry.

2. Knowledge of the prospect's industry, environment, and applications for the product or service.

3. Knowledge of how the product or service can benefit the prospect's business.

As a consultative seller you need to acquire and be prepared to share information and expertise on your own industry. This means providing prospects with an education on your industry's trends, where the industry is headed, who the major players are, how the industry works, and the ways the industry's products or services can improve their business.

You should also be prepared to critique your own industry, pointing out dysfunctions, downward trends, and any sloppy behaviors of the players. Sellers need to educate buyers on their organization's approach to the industry, strategic position, entire product and service offering, and what competitive advantages they enjoy.

It is not enough to offer expertise in your own industry. To position yourself as a consultative resource, you must also demonstrate knowledge of the prospect's industry — major trends, issues, pressures, and opportunities, as well as the general direction the industry is headed. A keen understanding of the prospect's industry is a key component of gaining attention and respect early in the sales process.

Educate Yourself

There are a variety of resources where you can find industry-specific knowledge. Industry research houses such as www.-firstresearch.com, www.business.com, www.factiva.com, and www.valuationresources.com offer current information on industry-specific trends, issues, and opportunities in vertical markets including finance, health care, insurance, government, education, retail, legal, and manufacturing.

You can also acquire industry knowledge by reading annual reports of the market leaders. In the first several pages, the president's letter to shareholders generally details the direction the industry is headed, the opportunities and challenges facing the company within that industry, and what the organization is doing to position itself to seize the opportunities and overcome the challenges. In order to gain a general understanding of specific industries you can also subscribe to industry periodicals, which can be found at www.freetradepubs.com and www.freetrademagzinesource.com.

You can also research industry specific trends at sources like Yahoo Finance, www.schwab.com, and www.Morningstar.com. Many vertical market sales professionals join industry associations and attend association conferences and seminars; these provide an opportunity to not only gain an in-depth understanding of the industry but to meet and interview industry experts and network with conference attendees.

Beyond general industry knowledge, consultative sellers need to be acutely familiar with the prospect's business model and the operating environment into which their product or service would be integrated.

By focusing on a specific industry (vertical market sales) over time, sellers gain not only an in-depth perspective of the general issues facing the industry but an understanding of how decisions are made and budgets are deployed. Combined with experience selling into a specific industry and specialized training in a vertical market, these elements give you a base of invaluable information and credibility.

Consultative sellers must also understand every aspect of their product or service—as well as their competition's products and services. Only this level of knowledge allows you to educate your prospect by thoroughly comparing and contrasting your offerings with each competitor's.

The nuance here lies in approaching prospects as an expert resource, enabling the prospect to become a better informed thus more confident decision maker.

Innovation

The second key to successful consulting is innovation. My new teacher defined this as "offering new ideas, methods, models, and tools that the prospect is not currently deploying but that are delivering proven results in similar organizations."

In my experience and research of buyers this view is 180 degrees opposite of how many sellers approach prospects. Often the typical sales approach is *rip and replace* or *upgrade,* not true innovation. IT sellers often rip out old boxes and replace them with new ones or upgrade the prospect's old system with a new one. While the replacement may offer some new *features* this approach is hardly consultative and is usually transactional and product price-centric, yielding little competitive distinction for the seller or long-term benefits for the buyer.

Consultants are trained to look at the prospective client's environment, current methods, models, tools, and technology with an open mind to creating new outcomes. The challenge here is often timing. Many times sellers and buyers engage only when the buyer is ready to replace one product, service program, or vendor with another.

Buyers often engage sellers after they have conducted an internal assessment of requirements and begun to evaluate competitive products or services and vendors. In this reactionary process, there is little room for innovation. The result is often a negligible improvement in productivity camouflaged by the glitter of expensive new equipment or services.

The Business-as-Usual Trap

Innovation can become nearly impossible once an incumbent vendor has settled into a maintenance role and *business-as-usual* behavior. At this stage, most discussions occur at the mid-management level, and account reviews focus on the client's original objectives. These often end up being status reports, not ventures into innovative territory. Generally, there is little emphasis on how the incumbent vendor can "notch it up" and scale positive results into other departments or divisions.

This is why timing is everything. Approaching prospects with the idea of innovating (versus simply expanding the status quo) is very difficult if the buyer is currently *in the market*, has gone through an internal assessment, and is to the point of gathering proposals. If your goal is to gain competitive distinction you must shift your strategy from simply submitting a me-too competitive proposal to submitting a completely unique proposal based on innovation.

This is precisely why the consultative sales model presented in *The $50 Ice Cream Cone* is best applied when the prospect is *not currently in the market* and competitors are not interfering in the process. This gives you a blank canvas and the opportunity to approach the prospect with the intent of truly innovating the environment.

Acceleration

Who was this wise old woman from whom I was getting such gold-plated advice? Turns out she sat on the board of directors of IBM! She explained that IBM hires many consultants, and before the board approves any prospective consultant's proposal they ask themselves two questions:

- What do they know that we don't know?

- What innovative models, methods, processes, or tools are they recommending that are already delivering results for other companies?

My new teacher went on to provide the third key to successful consulting—acceleration. She said that when the board of directors at IBM sits down to discuss a problem or issue there are a lot of smart people in the room. Given enough time, the board would solve any problem presented. If an outside consultant could help them solve the problem faster, thus saving time and money, they would gladly green light the proposal. This ability to enhance a company's internal problem-solving ability and save time and money is called acceleration.

Your prospects and clients will arrive where they want to go with or without your help. It may be through an internal education process, it may be one of your competitors who gets them there, or they might copy one of their own competitor's business models. The point is, it may as well be you who gets them where they want to go! It may as well be you who brings the expertise and innovation that improves their business model, reduces costs, increases value, or results in competitive advantage.

One aspect of acceleration is prediction. A prepared consultant knows the road ahead when it comes to implementing innovative solutions. Knowing where major speed bumps and breakdowns are most likely to occur and how to avoid them is of great value to any buyer. Knowing the best practices of other clients who have implemented similar solutions in similar environments also accelerates successful implementation.

It was just one year after I started my consulting business that I met this woman. When I got off the plane my eyes were wide open to a whole new way to approach my profession, clients, and prospects. After years of formal schooling and months of frustration building a consulting business, I had learned the true value that consultants bring to the table. Now let's take a look at how to link that paradigm and approach to a truly consultative sales behavior.

The Pure Play
Consulting Process

M ost every profession has a defined process, a step-by-step series of actions leading to a desired result. Typically the process is broken down into subsets with labels attached to each and specific tools designed to prompt and support implementation. Golfers, airline pilots, surgeons, lawyers, teachers, salespeople — even artists and musicians — have defined processes to help them successfully execute their profession.

Some professionals, such as airline pilots and surgeons, adhere strictly to their process because perfect implementation is a matter of life and death. Each step is thoroughly thought through, documented with checklists, and implemented without deviation. Other professionals such as golfers and musicians have a process, but often improvise and experiment in implementation.

In this section I will present what I refer to as the "pure play consulting process," which consultants are trained in at well-known business schools and big-time consulting firms.

Overview of the Pure Play Consulting Process

There are four steps in the pure play consulting process. I advise you to strive to apply each step rigorously but leave room for improvisation within the context of what you're selling. The idea is to link the traditional consulting process to a collaborative selling process, creating a balanced approach that adds value for the buyer and creates competitive distinction for the seller.

The four steps in the pure play consulting process are:

1. Analyze the prospective client's current state.

2. Design a new state founded on innovative solutions.

3. Implement the proposed recommendations and solutions.

4. Manage the implementation with an eye on measurement of results and continual improvement.

Analyze

The first step in the consulting process is to analyze the prospect's current state within the context of your expertise and product or service you are offering. Internally, this may include examining current methods, operating costs, total cost of ownership, business processes, facilities, employee attitudes, and management objectives and challenges. Externally, an analysis of the prospect's competitive position, customer attitudes, economic trends, and market pressures may be relevant.

A thorough analysis will usually reveal dysfunctions, wastes, redundancies, missed opportunities, out-of-control costs, flawed business processes, misconceptions, miscommunications, management shortfalls, areas where training needs to be improved, and areas ripe for innovation. It will also reveal good news, such as areas where current methods, tools, and processes are delivering extraordinary results, creating an opportunity to capture these *best practices* and scale them across the organization.

Design

Based on the analysis, your job is now to design a proposed state founded on your innovative recommendations. For every problem area, you as the consultant should offer innovative, customized solutions. The proposed state is the "after" picture in a before-and-after sequence.

It is here that you should propose improvements: new strategies, tactics, tools, resources, or technologies that enable your prospect to meet their objectives, overcome challenges, reduce or eliminate dysfunctions, improve business processes, and seize opportunities.

Implement

Remember, one of the keys to successful consulting is expertise. If consultants are worth their salt they will offer prospective clients guidance in effectively implementing the proposed solutions.

Because they have real-world experience in assisting other clients in implementing innovative solutions, consultants know where the speed bumps and breakdowns usually occur. This practical experience helps clients avoid these problems, thus accelerating successful implementation, saving time and money.

Manage

The last step is to manage implementation with the goal of measuring results and improving performance to maximize the customer's return on investment. Here, both you and the client measure the results delivered and validate the ROI. This process can reveal discrepancies, requiring adjustments in implementation until the desired results are consistently met.

As a part of this four-step process, the relationship between you and your client becomes more of a partnership, with the client taking ownership and responsibility for the implementation while you act as a resource for ongoing project management.

Before I present a detailed explanation of how to implement each step of the pure play consulting process I will first describe how you can create the opportunity to do so with a perspective client/buyer.

Getting Hired as the Consultant: The Initial Appointment

The focus here will be on linking the pure play consulting process with a collaborative sales process. Again, the objective is to enable sellers to combine consultative behavior with a sales process that creates a remarkable customer experience, resulting in a successful sale and long-term customer loyalty.

In order for the pure play consultative selling process to work sellers must approach prospective accounts at the top budget authority level. Generally, top-level managers are visionary, respectful of expertise, open-minded to innovative ideas, and eager to identify ways to improve results. As I said before, it's best to approach the top budget authority *when they are not currently in the market.*

In this book I defer discussion on the front-end steps of the sales process — including prospecting, pre-call planning, and building rapport and relationships — to *Power Selling*, where Chapter 3 addresses the setting of initial appointments with top-level decision makers via marketing letters and telephone prospecting. Later in this book I elaborate on methods for gaining and utilizing case studies in prospect development. Combined, these prospecting and marketing methods are proven to be effective in gaining an audience with top-level budget authority decision makers.

Let's assume the marketing ideas work in securing an initial appointment with the prospect. Here, I will present what to do on the initial appointment with top-level executives in order to capture their attention, hold their interest, and ultimately engage you as their consultant. It is your mission to transcend focusing on products and price, and focus on added value from the very first appointment.

The objectives of the initial appointment are to:

- Position yourself as an expert consultative resource.

- Present the pure play consultative process and the benefits the prospect gains from going through that process.

- Gain approval for implementing the process, beginning with analysis of the current state.

Here are the logistics and nuances of a successful initial appointment.

After your introduction and initial rapport-building conversation, I suggest you develop and deliver a 30-second call introduction that goes something like this.

At [your organization] we specialize in providing expertise, innovation, and accelerated results in the area of [your expertise/industry]. My role is to act as an advisor and a liaison and to engage prospective clients in our unique consulting process which includes four steps. First, we analyze your current state in the area of [your expertise/ industry] and document related processes, total cost of ownership, and areas for improvement. Then we design a proposed state with innovative recommendations based on our expertise, products, services, and solutions. Next, we collaborate with your management team in implementing any recommendations you approve. Finally, we measure initial results to validate your return on investment and identify areas to optimize implementation going forward. We also partner with your team to manage the project on an ongoing basis.

You can gain more information on developing a positioning statement in Chapter 5 of *Power Selling*.

Now that you've positioned yourself as a consultative resource, you must expand on that 30-second sound bite with a more specific and robust presentation of your consultative process. I suggest starting the presentation by demonstrating that you understand the industry-specific challenges facing the prospect by citing one or two from your research. Next, present a brief overview of the ways your company can help your prospect's organization overcome those challenges.

The heart of the presentation should include a comprehensive explanation of the pure play consulting process. First, simply expand on your 30-second introduction, filling in with specifics on exactly how you go about analyzing the client's current state. Then explain the benefits: that a thorough analysis generally reveals areas ripe for improvement. At this point explain that the best time to conduct an analysis is when the prospect is not actively in the market for the related products or services. This allows the analysis to be conducted in a more objective manner, free of the pressures of deadlines.

Next, describe how you design the proposed state based on your expertise and your company's innovative solutions. Here is where you flaunt your internal resources, experts, and strategic partners or vendors. Explain how your proposal will include recommendations that address the prospect's challenges, help eliminate dysfunctions, reduce costs, and position the prospect to seize opportunities.

The next phase of the presentation focuses on the process of implementing the recommendations. The central message is that you will act as a resource for the prospect's management team during implementation, passing ownership of the project to the prospect's internal team in the process.

Finally, present how you will measure initial results and validate initial return on investment. Beyond ROI, the measurement of initial results will reveal what was learned in the implementation and what adjustments need to be made going forward to optimize ROI. Here the consultant/seller also presents how they assist clients in managing the implementation on an ongoing basis.

Toward the end of the presentation but prior to closing, I suggest presenting one or two powerful case studies providing examples of how other clients progressed through the process and what benefits and results they realized.

The objective is simple: to close the prospect on hiring you as their consultative resource. Here, you may present the benefits of having an outsider—who has no need to protect territory and is not encumbered with internal politics—take a fresh look at this area of the business. You may explain that, generally, incumbent vendors fall into a "business-as-usual" mode and rarely conduct such an objective analysis for two reasons: reducing vendor costs is not in their interest, and they are afraid the analysis will reveal findings which will cast them in a poor light.

The Close

Close this presentation by promising that at the end of the process, whether you do business together or not, the prospect will become a better informed decision maker and come away with ideas that will enable them to overcome challenges and better seize opportunities.

At this point if the prospect asks "When can we get started?" or "How much does this process cost?" you know you've built remarkable value in your pure play consultative process.

Many salespeople ask me, "Should I charge the prospect for conducting the analysis and designing the proposed state?" In some cases charging professional fees for this service is normal and therefore expected. This is usually based on the scope of work and resources required. Typically, if the scope of work and required resources are not a huge investment, I suggest positioning the analysis and design steps as a value-add to your sales process.

Keep in mind, if you charge the prospect even a nominal amount, your analysis findings and recommendations become the property of the prospect. Now the prospect has the right to do with that information whatever they like — including handing it over to the incumbent vendor or a group of competitors as part of an RFP.

I suggest brokering a *fair exchange* agreement that binds you and the client in consideration of the time and resources invested in conducting the analysis and designing the recommendations. In presenting the fair exchange agreement, explain the investment of time and resources involved and put a monetary price tag on that investment. Now offer a fair exchange. Simply explain that, in lieu of charging the fees, you will invest the time and resources in exchange for three considerations:

- A nondisclosure agreement protecting the information from exposure to any outside audience.

- Full and timely access to all information required during the assessment.

- An executive audience to present the analysis findings and proposed recommendations of the newly designed state.

In my experience and that of many of my clients who have embraced this process, there is very little push back if the agreement is presented eloquently. We have, in fact, found that top-level executives are comfortable with nondisclosures and respectful of the time and resources invested by sellers to provide them with accurate and valuable decision support information. They also respect savvy business practices when they see them.

Determining Dependence

After gaining the approval to conduct the analysis, but prior to investing the time and resources, I suggest conducting a quick acid test to determine if the prospect's buying philosophy and behavior is price-, value-, or premium-centric.

Early in this book I presented the value pyramid model from a marketing perspective to help sellers understand how to add value and enhance the customer experience. I recommend presenting the same value pyramid model to prospective clients early in the sales process. By sharing this model with prospects and opening a dialogue on the relationship between value and price, you can ignite a provocative conversation that sets the stage for the entire consulting/sales process. After presenting the value pyramid simply explain where on the pyramid your organization operates in terms of marketing philosophy and business model. Next, turn the conversation to the prospect, asking him to identify where on the value pyramid his organization operates. In the course of the discussion, prospects will often reveal related buying behaviors that will tell you whether they are price-, value-, or premium-centric.

In my experience, opening this discussion early can be extremely productive in laying a foundation for a selling strategy going forward. If prospects view themselves as having a low dependence on the offering and reveal that they are price-centric, you can scale down the scope of your analysis accordingly to accelerate the sales process. If prospects view themselves as semi-dependent and more value-centric, you can justify the investment of time to determine what type of value-add they want and tailor a proposal that reflects the relationship between value and price. And if they see themselves as heavily dependent and premium-centric, then both seller and buyer can set the tone for a highly collaborative engagement, with sellers offering a premium customer experience and buyers expecting a premium price.

CHAPTER 5

Implementing the Pure Play Consulting Process

Step 1: Analyze the Prospective Client's Current State

Now that you've been hired as the consultant you can proceed to the first step in the process. Each seller's analysis process will differ depending on the products or services being sold. The extent of the analysis is also dependent on the seller's commitment to going beyond just matching a product or service to an obvious need, resulting in a short-term sale. Other considerations include the time and resources the seller has to devote to the analysis, the importance of the product or service to the prospect's core business, and obviously the potential sales revenue, profit, and commission. In my experience, the more comprehensive the analysis, the more that business issues needing resolution become obvious, leading to more opportunities to innovate and therefore more sales opportunities in the long term.

As with any step in the process, the analysis could (and in some cases should) be approached at first as a pilot program, then expanded in phases and ultimately scaled to the entire enterprise. With this approach, sellers and buyers can avoid becoming encumbered in an analysis that is too broad in scope, requiring enormous time and resources and yielding so much information that it could lead to paralysis in the end.

The Problem with Consultants and Their Analysis

Consultants are often viewed as threats from the outside by the client's mid-management. With this in mind you should strive to keep your analysis as non-intrusive as possible, being careful not to disturb managers, employees, vendors, or customers in the process.

Staying consistent with the concept that many sellers must collaborate with multiple decision makers, I will present here a discovery process designed to develop a comprehensive view of the prospect's current state from each decision maker's point of view.

The questioning method presented here gives you three positive outcomes. First, in the process of engaging and interviewing diverse decision makers and influencers, you will develop relationships deep and wide within the organization. Second, by asking diversified questions you will capture more diversified information which leads to more robust and diversified recommendations (selling opportunities). Third, based on the information, you can go on to craft more powerful presentations and more compelling proposals.

Following is a four-tiered discovery process designed to engage the four decision domains: Finance, Operations, Purchasing, and key department management. Again, the goal of the questioning is to enable sellers to capture information on the prospect's current state from a diverse perspective.

It makes sense to ask all four influencers the same questions initially and then drill deeper with *title-specific questions* based on the essential duties of the job and each individual's personal motivations. I present a partial list of suggested questions that should be asked of all decision makers and then a list of title-relevant questions for each.

Questions You May Want to Add to Your Existing Analysis

Sample Questions for All Four Tiers

- On a scale of 1 to 10, how mission-critical do you view our product/service to your organization? (1 = very low mission-critical, 10 = extremely mission-critical).

- What are your major objectives regarding managing [aspects of seller's product/service]?

- What are your major challenges regarding managing [aspects of seller's product/service]?

- What are your top-of-mind corporate initiatives currently being implemented?

- What are your most pressing business issues?

- Describe the top trends in your industry forcing you to change the way you do business.

- Who are your internal customers?

- What are their motivations?

- Who are your external customers?

- What are their motivations?

- What gets measured here?

- Describe your expectations from a vendor or partner.

In addition to these questions, you should ask questions that are relevant to the person's title and areas of responsibility. The information captured here enables sellers to identify local requirements and design a proposal that satisfies each influencer's needs and desires.

Sample questions for Finance and top management (tailored from the essential job activities and motivations on pages 38–40):

- Briefly describe your business model.

- What are your organization's biggest growth opportunities?

- What are your fastest growing brand/product/ service categories?

- Describe your next year's market expansion goals.

- Describe your major objectives regarding managing:
  - Budgets.
  - Vendors and contracts.
  - Complying with government regulations.
  - Managing operating cash.
  - Improving cash flow.
  - Streamlining vendors.

- Describe your major challenges regarding managing:
  - Budgets.
  - Vendors and contracts.
  - Complying with government regulations.
  - Managing operating cash.
  - Improving cash flow.
  - Streamlining vendors.

- What gets measured in Finance?
  - Total cost of ownership.
  - Economic value-add.
  - Return on investment.

- How are executives measured?

- What are your future areas of integration or consolidation?

- How do you go about identifying cost synergies?

- What is your experience in having outside resources conduct analysis? What was the result?

- Who are your strategic partners?

- What are they doing that is powerful?

Sample questions for Operations (tailored from the essential job activities and motivations on pages 41–42):

- Describe your major objectives regarding managing:
  - Facilities.
  - Vendors.
  - Technology.
  - Employees.

- Describe your major challenges regarding managing:
  - Facilities.
  - Vendors.
  - Technology.
  - Employees.

- Describe your challenges in developing accurate budgets for:
  - Space.
  - Equipment.
  - Furnishings.
  - Support personnel.
  - Security.
  - Maintenance.

- Describe your initiatives to:
  - Simplify business processes.
  - Streamline communications between managers and employees.
  - Create a quality work environment.
  - Meet internal customers' expectations.

■ What gets measured in Operations?
  – Vendor performance.
  – Employee productivity.
  – Technology performance.
  – Internal customer satisfaction.
  – External customer satisfaction.

Sample questions for Purchasing (tailored from the essential job activities and motivations on pages 45–47):

■ Describe your major objectives regarding managing:
  – Vendors.
  – Contracts.
  – Costs.
  – Internal customers.

■ Describe your major challenges regarding managing:
  – Vendors.
  – Contracts.
  – Costs.
  – Internal customers.

■ How do you go about validating proposals?
  – Best product/service.
  – Vendor capabilities.
  – Best price/value ratio.

■ Do you have a formal vendor selection criteria?

■ What strategic partnerships have you developed?

■ Which of those are most powerful and why?

■ What gets measured in Purchasing?
  – Operating costs.
  – Total cost of ownership.
  – Related costs.

■ Describe how you evaluate vendors:
  – RFP/bid comparison.
  – Visitation of vendor's facilities.
  – Interviews of vendor's management team.
  – Interviews of vendor's references.

■ Describe your satisfaction level with your current vendor.

■ What desired improvements would you like to see?

■ When was the current vendor in last to:
  – Analyze current methods to improve.
  – Identify areas to reduce costs.
  – Share latest industry trends and technology.

■ Describe your contractual obligation with your current vendor.

■ Describe the decision-making process.

■ What is your time frame for making a decision and awarding the business?

■ What needs to happen between now and then?

■ What is the source for the budget?

■ Is the budget approved?

Sample questions for key department management (tailored from the essential job activities and motivations on pages 48–49):

■ Describe your major objectives in regard to managing [aspects of seller's product/service]?

■ Describe your major challenges in regard to managing [aspects of seller's product/service]?

■ Describe your satisfaction level with your current methods for [applications of seller's product/service]?

■ What gets measured in your department?

■ How do you go about evaluating your department's requirements for [seller's product/service]?

■ How do you justify your budgets in Purchasing, Finance, and Operations?

■ Rate your current methods in meeting your internal customers' expectations for value, service, and quality.

Be prepared to wordsmith and add questions according to the prospect you're meeting with and the products or services being offered.

Nuances to Discovery

You may be thinking "I'm not too keen on sitting down with a list of questions and conducting a clinical interview with all these people. It just doesn't look smooth."

I agree there is danger in coming across as intrusive and mechanical. Obviously one cannot just march in dressed in a white smock with a clipboard, stopwatch, and lengthy list of questions and interview the decision team en masse. At the same time, think about the last time you sat down face to face with a professional such as an attorney, physician, tax preparer, or contractor. Did that person invest ample time with you to completely understand your current situation and your objectives and challenges? Were they composed and organized in their approach to capturing valid information that would equip them to argue your case effectively, diagnose and treat your condition properly, prepare your tax returns with your best interest in mind, or remodel your kitchen exactly the way you envisioned?

Based on my experience you will find that executives generally expect this approach and respect the professional who engages in a formal discovery process that gives the appearance of interest, thoroughness, and a commitment to "getting it right." This formal discovery process lends you credibility and builds trust as both parties participate and work together towards the same outcome.

My first suggestion for conducting an effective analysis is not a nuance but an absolute must. You must have sponsorship from the top-level decision maker. The top-level executive must provide a formal introduction to the rest of the decision makers and influencers. This introduction must present you as a collaborative resource who is helping the executive identify areas to innovate.

Before delving into an interview, you must build a strong rapport with each participant, putting them at ease and making them comfortable sharing information. After you build rapport you must create a perception of value in the analysis. I have found that showing each participant a sample deliverable or case study helps the person being interviewed see the value in sharing information. Simply explain to each person involved that they have a role in documenting the company's current state and a voice in designing and implementing the newly designed state.

During your interviews it helps to have the curiosity of a six-year-old. Couple that curiosity with the art of questioning like a seasoned therapist. Have the questions formatted onto a prompter so you can stay focused, yet you must have total command of the questions so you can articulate them clearly and conversationally. Keep in mind that the interview is just that: an interview, not a sales call. Resist the temptation to present any potential recommendations along the way.

One of the most challenging aspects of conducting interviews is taking copious notes. Good therapists are trained in the technique of delayed note-taking and maintaining eye contact in order to keep the conversation alive. Remember, the more critical information gathered here, the more robust and customized the subsequent proposal, presentation, and closing argument will be.

Step 2: Design an Innovative Proposed State

The second step in the pure play consulting process is designing a proposed state founded on your recommendations. For every area of objectives and challenges not met, dysfunction, waste, redundancy, and opportunities missed, your mission is to offer innovative, customized solutions.

Here consultants apply their expertise to propose new strategies, tactics, tools, resources, and technology that enable prospects to overcome challenges and seize opportunities. The newly designed state of business operations obviously includes your products, services, or programs as critical components of achieving these outcomes.

Designing a proposed state cannot be done in a vacuum or the sanitary confines of the consultant's office. This step demands high collaboration between you and your prospect.

What Sellers Can Learn from Architects

A few years ago I bought a 30-year-old house in a marina development on the Southern California coast and engaged in a year-long renovation project. In working with architects, engineers, contractors, and tradesmen it became obvious that starting out with a vacant lot with no existing structure would have been easier than endeavoring a major remodel.

In the design phase, architects and engineers had to work around existing infrastructure, the original designer's ideas, and the original owner's taste, all of which created built-in inhibitors and significant challenges to innovation. One thing I learned in the design phase was the importance and value of collaboration between all parties involved, not only in the design but the construction (implementation) phase as well. While the architects and I provided the conceptual ideas, it was the engineers, contractors, tradesmen, and even laborers who provided early expertise as to which ideas were most practical to implement.

Just like architects, consultative sellers must engage the prospective client's top management, decision influencers, internal customers, and sometimes existing vendors to gain valuable practical insights during the design phase. Consultative sellers should also bring other expert resources to the table in the design phase—vendors, contractors, and suppliers—to ensure that what is being designed can be seamlessly and smoothly delivered by all involved.

Collaboration in the design phase also allows your prospect to take ownership of both the problem areas and the recommendations. It gives prospects an opportunity to get their fingerprints on the design of the proposed state and encourages participation early in the implementation. While collaborating, prospects begin to internalize and accept the proposed state, paving the way for a smooth implementation.

At this stage, you must walk a fine line between innovation and preservation. Often, you must work with your prospect's current infrastructure and the built-in inhibitors. It is here the consultative seller's expertise and judgment is applied to breaking barriers that inhibit innovation.

Two Win/Win Case Studies

Here are two examples of applying the pure play consultative sales process and adding value to a product to create a customer experience that pushes the seller up the value/profit pyramid.

A client of mine is in the medical laboratory products and supplies business. The products in this industry are commonly viewed as commodities and the buyers are typically price-centric, and so the sales process is generally low-touch and transactional. The seller is nothing more than a common vendor.

During the analysis phase of the pure play consulting process, my client identified challenges in a prospect's procurement process which created painful inventory problems. Further analysis revealed cost inefficiencies and an inordinate amount of human involvement to assure that internal customers were satisfied.

Instead of just proposing discounted products, the seller added value and totally changed the customer's current state by providing a complimentary service that included taking over the management of the customer's entire supply room. In addition, the seller streamlined the customer's procurement and supply chain processes to assure just-in-time delivery, consolidated and leveraged the customer's buying power to reduce costs, and enabled the customer to redeploy current human resources to more mission-critical assignments. In this case the seller solved the customer's problems, shifted the focus from product and price to solutions, and increased the average transaction value and profits as a result.

Another example was provided to me by a lumber salesman. When I asked him how his sales process had changed in his more than 30 years of selling lumber, he explained that by reinventing his sales process he was able to create a value-added customer experience, enabling him to transcend the typical transactional sale of a commodity.

For years, lumber salespeople would simply show up at a

lumber yard and say, "We have some two-by-fours on sale, how many can you take?" or "We're overstocked on redwood posts so we're offering a promotional discount, how many can I ship?" Under a pure play consultative process, the salesperson now visits the lumberyard and determines the existing inventory of lumber products. He then analyzes the customer's historical sales receipts and with predictive modeling determines exactly when the lumber yard will run out of specific products. Next, the seller projects when the lumber yard should place an order for those products to avoid running out of stock and risking losing customers to competitors.

Again, this proves a win/win for both the seller and buyer. The seller resolved the customer's business issues via innovation which was only possible through the seller's in-depth understanding of the customer's applications, challenges, and business model.

These two examples also demonstrate that by implementing a consultative and collaborative sales process that addresses the client's business issues, the seller can transcend the status of a vendor and leap to partner status.

The Deliverable and Consensus Meeting

Once the analysis is completed and the newly designed state is ready to propose, it is the consultant's role to package the analysis findings and recommendations into a *consultative deliverable*. This is a document that prompts and supports discussion, debate, and collaboration — ultimately leading to action-planning the implementation of the consultant's recommendations.

The deliverable may include flow charts, diagrams and other visuals of the prospect's current state and the same for the proposed state. It may include a cost analysis of current spending compared to proposed spending. In my practice, the deliverable is not a full-scale financial proposal. It does not include exact specifications and pricing on the proposed new products and services, but offers enough detail to establish a credible business case for moving forward to the financial proposal phase once management has embraced the general recommendations.

The deliverable is presented in a face-to-face meeting prior to the delivery of a formal financial proposal. This meeting is referred to as a *consensus meeting*, because its key objective is to reach consensus that the information in the deliverable is valid. The meeting also creates an opportunity to dialogue and collaborate on the potential of implementing the recommendations.

The heart of this strategy is to get your prospect *prioritizing your recommendations* and becoming involved in implementing your solutions before you even deliver your formal proposal. By collaborating with your prospects to identify which of your recommendations *they* want to implement first (thus which of your recommendations they want proposed), you exponentially improve your chances of having your financial proposal accepted.

In consulting we call this "phasing in the solutions." Phase one is to implement the top three to four solutions over a reasonable time frame and measure the results. Phase two, upon confirmation of results, is to implement the next three or four prioritized solutions, and so on, until all the solutions are implemented over time.

Phasing in solutions gives your prospect a chance to implement manageable projects without assuming the financial risk associated with drastic, abrupt changes. This process also helps you initially implement a manageable scope of work and deliver quick results. This leads to greater credibility, trust, and acceptance in implementing subsequent phases.

When presenting the consultative deliverable at the consensus meeting, engage your prospect in discussing your findings and the problem areas which the analysis revealed, asking which of the problems are critical, or "must solve now," which would classify as "solve in phase two," which fall in the category of "solve in phase three," and so on.

Also engage your prospect in discussing how you will work together to implement the recommended solutions. If applicable, explain how you and your support team will work with the prospect's management team to implement the solutions.

Once you've reviewed the newly designed state and your recommended solutions, revisit the prioritization list. Suggest that, based on this collaboration, you will offer a financial proposal on the *top-priority* solutions.

This is where patience comes into the picture. One strategy is to be prepared to scale down your initial scope of work and your initial proposal to the top three or four priorities, get those solutions implemented, measure your effectiveness, and return every 90 to 120 days to review your results and then prioritize the next three to four recommendations. A second strategy is to propose and gain commitment on the entire host of recommendations and phase them in over time.

In a way, your deliverable acts as a proposal for the financial proposal. It sets you up for presenting a final proposal that hits the target spot-on. It gets prospects engaged and committed to owning their problems and solving their problems with your solutions.

At the end of the consensus meeting and deliverable presentation I suggest you present a proposed *implementation agenda*. This allows you to collaborate with the prospect on the logistical process for implementing your recommendations. It also helps you open the discussion as to how and when you intend to close the sale.

On your implementation agenda, simply list the steps both organizations—buyer and seller—will need to take to successfully implement your recommendations. By identifying the steps in sequence and attaching realistic time frames for each, you are pacing your prospect through future events that will lead to the sale.

The first step is the review of the analysis findings and the newly designed state at the consensus meeting. The date attached is obviously the date you present your deliverable to the prospect. The next step is for you and your prospect to prioritize the recommendations your prospect wants to implement. The date attached is the same as your consensus meeting and deliverable presentation date. The next step is the presentation of your financial proposal for the products and services encompassed in your prioritized solutions. The date attached is ideally within a few days of the consensus meeting. The next step listed is that your prospect must approve the proposal. Just to make things interesting, attach the same date as the presentation of your proposal.

Crafting and Delivering the Financial Proposal

In this section I share an abbreviation of the elements of winning proposals from *Power Selling* that will accelerate getting favorable decisions from your prospects. Of course, these proposals will itemize product and service specifications, include pricing, and describe terms and conditions of the transaction as any proposal should. But instead of focusing on products, services, and pricing, we're going to stay the course and focus on *proposing recommendations that help prospects meet their objectives and resolve business issues.* We're then going to *cost justify* those recommendations with a compelling proposal.

In the first section of your proposal, you should briefly restate the primary objectives and challenges that your proposal will address. Then provide a findings page that summarizes the customer's current state, listing the downsides and pain points.

Next provide a cost analysis section. I find that cost analysis is easiest to present in a simple side-by-side format. First, itemize your prospect's current itemized costs on the left side of the page, and then list your proposed itemized solutions on the right side. For both the current costs and proposed costs, list all the elements of operating costs, or *total cost of ownership*. If your proposal includes some of these costs, make sure you indicate it here. For example, if your proposal includes customer support, itemize it and simply insert "included" in the space for this line item. I never use the words "no charge" or "free," as they diminish the value of your inclusions.

At the conclusion of your side-by-side comparison, you have the opportunity to identify either an increase or decrease in total operating costs or total costs of ownership. If your prospect expenses these costs monthly, then finish this section with a total monthly increase or decrease in expenses, whichever is applicable.

If you are decreasing the prospect's expenses, thus saving money, then you will want to maximize that savings into an annual amount or even expand it over the life of the agreement. If you are increasing the prospect's expenses, then it's your job to *sell the difference* between what the prospect is currently paying and the proposed costs of your solutions. Selling the difference is sometimes as simple as listing the additional value and benefits the prospect receives for the additional outlay of costs. Here it makes sense to offer a simple summary of the benefits the prospect will realize from implementing the recommendations

The next section of the proposal may be titled "Solutions, Specifications, and Support." Introduce your specific recommendations, products, and services in detail. Include specifications, descriptions of your support and customer service programs, guarantees, warranties, installation, training services, etc.

Next, present an acquisition offer that explains how your customer can go about acquiring the products and services proposed. It is in this section that you will present your financial options, financing terms, fee-based a la carte items, and the terms of your proposal. You may also include a description of any value-added inclusions that you have bundled into your proposal.

The last page of the proposal should be the implementation agenda that was agreed upon at the conclusion of the consensus meeting. Revisiting that agenda here and now leads to a natural approval of the proposal and closing of the sale, and opens a collaborative dialogue as to how both organizations will go about implementing the specifics of the proposal. This is the next stage in the pure play consulting process, and the one that brings all your skills and expertise into play. In other words, next is the stage that separates the partners from the vendors.

On the following pages you will find a sample proposal from a company in the document technology sector which follows the format presented here.

A Document Technology Solution Proposal
for
Advantech

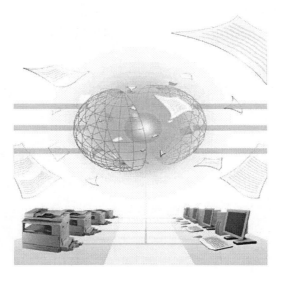

Prepared By:

Today's Document Solutions

Today's Document Solutions

Mr. Philip Michaels   July 7, 2007

Chief Financial Officer

Advantech

Dear Mr. Michaels

Thank you for the opportunity to consult and collaborate on the issues of document technology for Advantech. I appreciate your participation and contribution in the process that has led to my submission of the attached proposal.

This proposal will offer information and insights relative to Advantech's objectives for changing document technology, and Advantech's current document technology scenario. Based on this information, Today's Document Solutions will present our best suited Solutions accompanied by a financial analysis comparing the current and proposed methods.

Today's Document Solutions will then propose cost effective acquisition options, summarize the benefits of this proposal, offer an implementation agenda, and provide relative supporting documentation.

This proposal will provide a road map for implementing the proposed solutions by identifying the steps each organization must take in order to successfully meet Advantech's objectives and deliver the benefits promised in the proposal.

I look forward to presenting our solutions, reviewing the financial offer and discussing the logistics of implementation. I encourage your input as to how we can work together toward a favorable decision and a long-term working relationship.

Best Regards,

Steven Power

Print Management Specialists

Today's Document Solutions

Discovery Findings

Advantech's objectives regarding managing document technology are:

* Identify, track and control all output devices with a reporting system that will enable Advantech to account for all devices and internally recover related operating costs

* Partner with a vendor who will provide optimum reliability while offering a combined approach of technology, service, performance guarantees and systems for accountability.

* Partner with a single vendor that would provide all document delivery systems. The main objective is consistency in service, pricing, programs for acquiring, invoicing and supporting our document environment.

Advantech's challenges identified in managing document technology are:

* Lack of a reporting system that allows us to identify, track, and therefore control the cost of documents. We do not know what we have, what we are doing or what our costs are.

* "Acquisition of technology is out of control. Departments are purchasing printers *under the radar*; we have no idea of how many we have." Copiers are from multiple vendors with inconsistent costs and obligations, fax are from yet another vendor, printers and supplies from another. Managing the vendor list is time consuming and leads to lack of vendor accountability.

* Impacts include a collection of often poor performing devices from a variety of vendors, too many invoices, inconsistent pricing and service support and lack of control of who buys what from whom.

Today's Document Solutions

Based on Today's Document Solutions' discovery Advantech's current document environment is as follows:

__44__ Printers __6__ MFPs __14__ Ink Jet __7__ Color Printers

Your volume is broken down as follows:

396,000	Pages per month on printers	Monthly costs	$	11,880.00
72,000	Pages per month on MFPs	Monthly costs	$	1,656.00
3,750	Pages per month on Ink Jets	Monthly costs	$	2,022.00
18,400	Pages per month on color printers	Monthly costs	$	4,600.00
2,820	Pages per month outsourced	Monthly costs	$	1,100.00
492,970	Total pages per month			

Advantech's current total monthly operating costs are: $ 21,258.00

Comments on Current Situation

- Advantech has an average of four toner cartridges in every workgroup causing end user confusion and time consuming management of inventory by purchasing and department managers.
- Advantech has seven current vendors for document technology services resulting in diluted purchasing power and lack of vendor accountability.
- IT is spending an inordinate amount of time managing printer related issues.
- End users are purchasing color ink cartridges "under radar" at prices of up to $99 per cartridge for printers that originally cost $90.
- Many printers are either over or under utilized.
- Many workgroups have copiers, faxes and printers which are not connected to the network forcing end users to walk from device to device to produce and distribute documents. This fragmented process inhibits personal and workgroup productivity
- Valuable office space is being consumed by multiple document devices and related supply storage.
- Advantech currently has several outdated devices which are unreliable causing chaos in some workgroups and leading to the outsourcing of document production.
- Catalogs are currently outsourced at a premium cost. Due to constant changes in content, catalogs cannot be printed in volume which would bring the cost down.
- Advantech is currently paying a courier service to distribute documents to branch offices, vendors and customers at a premium expense.

Today's Document Solutions

Operating Costs Analysis

<u>Current Operating Costs</u>   <u>Proposed Operating Costs</u>

Document Production	Monthly Costs	Document Production	Monthly Costs
Printers Mono	11,880.00	Printers Mono	9,108.00
MFPs	1,656.00	MFPs	1,656.00
Ink Jets	2,022.00	Ink Jets	0.00
Color Printers	4,600.00	Color Printers	0.00
		New Color MFPs	3,980.00
Outsourced Documents	1,100.00	Outsourced Documents	0.00
Total Current Costs	**21,258.00**	**Total Proposed Costs**	**14,744.00**

Monthly Decrease   **$6,514.00**
Annual Decrease   **$78,168.00**

Total saving over term   **$312,672.00**

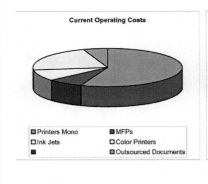

Current Operating Costs

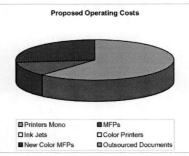

Proposed Operating Costs

Description of Proposed Solutions

The two Multi-functional devices proposed here will enable Advantech to consolidate print volumes onto more productive and cost effective devices. These devices will replace seven color printers, fourteen ink jet printers and allow for documents currently being outsourced at a premium to be produced on demand, in-house at a fraction of the cost.

Multi-function Workgroup Solutions

HP Color LaserJet 4730 MFP

Combine multiple functions--print, copy, scan-to-e-mail, analog fax, and digital sending with fast speeds in black-and-white and color, optional output capabilities, and reliable LaserJet technology - watch productivity soar.

 Get more done. Print color and black-and-white documents at speeds up to 31 pages per minute.
 Take a break from reloading paper. The HP Color LaserJet 4700 series printer offers an amazing input capacity of up to 2,600 sheets.
 Print short-run color documents in-house, quickly and affordably. When you print materials in-house, you have control over the process: *you* ensure that printing is effective, efficient, and affordable. Printing frequently updated materials on-demand, such as promotional material or brochures, means that you can make changes at a moments notice and never waste printed material due to obsolete information.

HP Color LaserJet 9500mfp

Get multiple functions and incredible results from one device. With color printing, copying, scanning-to-email, analog black- and-white faxing, and document finishing standard in one device.

 Save valuable time. Produce basic business documents and complex marketing materials at full engine speed—up to 24 pages per minute (ppm) in color or monochrome, single-sided or double-sided on a variety of paper sizes and types.
 Finish the job in-house. Choose one of four finishing options for office documents or professional color production: HP 8-bin mailbox, HP 3,000-sheet stapler/stacker, HP 3,000-sheet stacker, or HP 1,000-sheet multifunction finisher.
 Produce finished documents with the touch of a button. Experience a new level of flexibility with multiple document finishing options and tabloid paper capability. Use corner-stapling, folding, or saddlestitching to produce professionally finished documents or impressive marketing pieces.

Today's Document Solutions

Managed Print Services Program

Today's Document Solutions will provide a fully integrated managed print services program for Advantech's legacy printer fleet on an all inclusive agreement covering parts, labor and consumables.

The Managed Print Services Program will enable Advantech to reduce it's number of vendors from seven to two, reduce IT's involvement in managing printer related problems, provide consistent pricing and service support and increase vendor accountability.

Today's Document Solutions will provide an automated tracking and reporting system that will allow Advantech to account for all devices and related operating cost and recover those costs from each department.

The managed print program proposed here will enable Advantech to streamline and facilitate:
- Supply ordering
- Service consumables management
- Help desk support
- Preventative maintenance
- Life cycle management

Service Support

Responsive Service by Skilled Technicians: Our technical support professionals average 17 years in the industry. Every service technician completes a rigorous factory and in-house training curriculum. This on-going education ensures that they keep pace with advancing technology.

With more technicians per machine than any other local company, you can count on Today's Document Solutions for prompt and efficient service. Our service technicians are backed by a state-of-the-art dispatching system that enables a technician to be dispatched from the location nearest you. Our customers experience an average response time of under four hours. TDS's technicians are measured on machine reliability, not number of calls per day. As a result, our customers experience unparalleled manufacturer direct service and support.

Value-add programs

TDS will provide consulting services to assure the optimization of Advantech's print assets. We will identify and redeploy over / under utilized printers and route print jobs to most application appropriate device

TDS will act as Advantech's IT Help Desk via e-mail, telephone or onsite support which will free up IT to focus on core competencies.

TDS will provide preventative maintenance on all devices on a routine basis assuring optimum performance and longevity resulting in a maximum return on investment on each asset.

TDS will offer end-user training upon installation and on an ongoing basis to assure users maximize the functionality and productivity of each device.

TDS will offer a like-for-like loaner of any legacy printer deemed to need servicing at our facility.

Acquisition Offer

Print per page program on proposed technology:

All proposed models of print devices will be provided on a print-per-page program that includes the device, all service and all consumables for .023 per page for B&W and .19 for color. This program does not increase current expenditures yet provides the benefits of Multi-functional devices connected to Advantech's network.

Managed Print Services Program on Legacy Printer Fleet

TDS will provide the Managed Print Services for .023 per page for mono prints regardless of which printer prints and .19 per page for color.

Terms of Proposal

TDS will acquire meter reads from all devices monthly and generate a single invoice itemizing all devices, print volumes and per-page fees. Invoices will be payable upon receipt.

The term of the agreement is 48 months.

Benefits Summary

By implementing the proposed solutions Advantech will realize the following benefits:

- By placing new MFPs Advantech will realize Improved productivity and reduced operating cost via consolidation of:
  - Number of capital expenditures for copiers/printer/fax/scanner
  - Number of vendors related to copying, printing, faxing, scanning
  - Number of consumables (toner cartridges) requiring management
  - Amount of office space dedicated to document technology
  - Number of human steps involved in producing and distributing documents

- The Managed Print Services Value Proposition – Top Ten Benefits
  1. Know the cost of printing (Variable cost)
  2. Stabilize the cost of printing (Fixed cost)
  3. Proactively budget for printing
  4. Reduce costs via avoiding high cost of per call service
  5. Simplify supply inventory management
  6. Streamline accounts payable process
  7. Consolidate vendors = accountability & purchasing power
  8. Optimize printer performance & extend life = ROI
  9. Bundled contracts free up capital for core investments & improves cash flow
  10. Simplify IT help desk support

Implementing the recommendations proposed here will allow Advantech to meet the objectives stated by management regarding managing document technology:

- Identify, track and control all output devices with a reporting system that will enable Advantech to account for all devices and internally recover related operating costs

- Partner with a vendor who will provide optimum reliability while offering a combined approach of technology, service, performance guarantees and systems for accountability.

- Partner with a single vendor that would provide all document delivery systems. The main objective is consistency in service, pricing, programs for acquiring, invoicing and supporting our document environment.

- This proposal will allow Advantec to eliminate obsolete, high TCO color and ink Jet printers and replace them with multifunctional technology resulting in increased productivity and reduced Total Cost of Ownership. It also allows the in-house production of marketing brochures resulting in flexibility and reduced costs of outsourcing.
  - $3,930 per month
  - $47,160 per year
  - $188,640 over the term of the proposal

Step 3: Implement the Proposed Recommendations and Solutions

Consultants are the target of many jokes, some of which reflect the perception that consultants are merely theoretical *idea people* and not real-world implementers.

As I sit watching elaborate presentations of newly designed solutions offered by consultants, it often becomes painfully obvious that many recommended ideas, strategies, and tactics roll off the tongue more easily than is warranted. During these presentations I cringe when I hear a consultant say, "All you have to do is simply . . ." It quickly becomes clear that the planning, preparation, groundbreaking, and logistics most initiatives require — and the chain reaction of impacts and side effects down the line — are seldom understood by people sitting in a sanitized conference room.

In the implementation phase, things can get messy. Managers can get uptight and territorial. Both internal and external stakeholders can get confused and frustrated. Logistics can get scrambled and the introduction of new methods can cause unexpected delays and breakdowns in the very processes that they were intended to improve. Much like remodeling a house, time frames can get pushed out and budgets expanded, resulting in strained relations with the contractor, in this case the consultant.

This is where the true value of the consultant becomes apparent. Earlier I presented the three keys to successful consulting and expertise was number one. Hopefully the consultant's expertise is derived from real-world experience. The word experience literally means "practice through which knowledge or skill is gained" and "a series of events undergone or *lived through*." Expertise via experience is precisely what prospects and clients are hoping and paying for and the main reason they engage consultants.

Making Implementation Work

Throughout the implementation phase the consultative seller's role is that of a resource to the client's implementation team, not an actual team member. It is critical that clients take ownership of the newly designed state early in the process and put their signature on the project. This way when the inevitable speed bumps and transition pain manifest, the client's team is more prone to solve problems instead of becoming critical and resistant to the new methods, products, or services. Getting the client's team involved teaches them the nuances of converting over to new systems and helps them embrace change.

If you as the seller need to take a more dominant role in the implementation, I recommend having your implementation team leader partner with the client's implementation team leader as co–project managers.

Both co–project managers should collaborate to develop a comprehensive implementation and project management plan. This should include defining and documenting the roles and responsibilities of all team members and resources, and a communication protocol. Both organizations need to determine who is responsible for each aspect of implementation and formally establish who, when, and how members will communicate with one another throughout the process.

The project management plan should also include a defined process for conducting periodic project reviews. Naturally the frequency of project reviews is based on the scope and complexity of the project. If the project is large and complex, weekly or monthly reviews may be appropriate. In smaller, simpler projects reviews should be conducted monthly or semi-annually at a minimum.

A key to implementation of sizable initiatives that require considerable resources and have a major impact on the organization is to take it slow. Things can get overwhelming in the implementation phase on the enterprise level and consultants must be careful not to encourage too much implementation too fast.

In implementing comprehensive initiatives, consultants will often recommend a pilot, phase, and scale approach. The pilot step enables all parties to start implementing the recommendations in a controlled environment that is reflective of the enterprise. This allows each party to experience implementation and the nuances of the transition, gaining insight along the way.

After piloting, all parties can sit back, analyze the results and initial ROI, and use that information to make adjustments in the next step. During the pilot stage, the consultant's expertise should become evident and the prospect's internal buy-in more secure.

Ideally, the initial results will validate a positive ROI. This normally leads to an acceleration of the next step, the phasing in of recommendations in other departments, divisions, or locations, and then to the scaling of the recommendations enterprise-wide.

As you can see, collaboration is the key to successful implementation. The goal is to ensure that the new products or services will yield the maximum return on investment for the client. This process also assures the buyer that you will deliver on promises made along the way. In addition, it makes the buying partner responsible for fully embracing the new solutions and taking an active role in getting things started on the right foot, leading to a win/win implementation.

After a successful implementation some consultants part ways, or clients feel secure enough to go it alone. This is a mistake from either side. Let's look at why.

Step 4: Measure, Improve, and Manage

This final step in the pure play consulting process is the key to optimizing results and ROI. It is also the key for you, the consultant, to *staying alive*, keeping the relationship intact, and earning the right to start the process all over again, looking for new areas in which to innovate. Instead of disconnecting after successful implementation, you should work to stay on with clients — helping measure initial results, further improve implementation, and managing the project on an ongoing basis.

Measure Initial Results

During the original analysis of the client's current state, you measured various aspects of the operation in quantifiable terms. This analysis also revealed areas of dysfunction, missed opportunities, unresolved challenges, and objectives missed.

The design of the proposed state and the financial proposal included promises of quantifiable results that the client could expect from implementing the proposed recommendations. In most cases your financial proposal was cost-justified and approved by your buyer based on these expected results.

In this step of the process, the seller and buyer agree in advance what components of the proposal will be measured *after* implementation and when and how often the measurements will occur.

As each phase of the *initial implementation* is completed, both the consultant and client measure the results delivered by the products, services, and programs implemented and validate the ROI. In the process, discrepancies may appear, requiring adjustments in implementation until the desired results are consistently met.

Improve Implementation

The ongoing measurement of results will naturally lead to the constant drive to improve product or service performance and implementation by both parties. In the process, both buyer and seller are also constantly looking for areas where results are exceeding expectations. The idea here is to discover *best practices* that can be duplicated elsewhere.

Ideally these internal success stories will contain quantifiable results which, if properly documented, go a long way towards gaining credibility for the client's implementation team. They will take the credit!

Capturing success stories also goes a long way in validating the client's return on investment with top-level decision makers. This practice creates an opportunity to expand your reach in the account by leading to an expanded analysis that could reveal even more areas where you can help the client achieve more positive change.

Manage the Project on an Ongoing Basis

On an ongoing basis the consultant becomes a project management resource, assisting the client in managing and optimizing the now fully implemented recommendations. Over time the relationship between consultant and client becomes a partnership, with the client taking more ownership and internal responsibility for the implementation.

As a project management resource, you should be constantly accessible to the client's implementation team via both informal conversations and formal account reviews. You should always be ready to lend expertise and share methodology and best practices from other clients that could apply to this client's implementation.

It's All About Balance

As I stated early in this chapter, many salespeople and organizations practice consultative selling to some degree. In my experience working with hundreds of sales organizations, most benefit enormously by developing, practicing, and placing more emphasis on a formal consultative model and end up selling more as a result.

You may ask, "Why take the long, steep road of the pure play consultative process when it extends the sales process and adds complexity? Why not behave like the competition and go for the fast slam dunk and then move onto the next deal?" Here are a few sound reasons for going the distance.

First, as Warren Buffett would say, the pure play consultative process helps build a *moat* around your newly acquired customer, protecting it from your competition. During the process, both buyer and seller invest substantial time and effort in not only creating a solution but establishing a partnership.

Once the partners settle into their roles and develop a track record for delivering results, the quality of the relationship deepens and severely inhibits a competitor's ability to penetrate the account. In this scenario ongoing revenues and profits are protected and your opportunity to expand within the account becomes an automatic sequential step.

The pure play consultative process is not for every sales organization or prospect. Not every prospect makes a great partner. Price-centric buying organizations will not generate a return on investment on time, effort, and resources because you'll always be considered just a vendor. Most of my clients implement the pure play consultative process with value- and premium-centric prospects. These prospects may represent only 20 to 30% of the target accounts in the marketplace but it is not unusual that this small pool of prospects generates 60 to 80% of the most profitable sales revenues once acquired.

At the same time sellers must be careful not to become fixated on consulting and forsake selling. That's what this book is all about—balancing a formal consulting process with a collaborative selling process, resulting in outrageous value for the customer and increased sales for the seller.

The goal is to strike a perfect balance in both processes, bringing value to the prospect. Sellers who perfectly balance both the consulting and selling processes will gain competitive distinction over those who limit their analysis to a narrow scope, offer generic "rip and replace" or upgrade recommendations, and those whose idea of implementation is to take an order, cash the check, and high-five the customer, only to be seen again at contract renewal time.

The Business Case for Case Studies

Leveraging Successful Implementations

Almost every business invests in and therefore sees a value in corporate brochures, websites, and campaigns to espouse their marketing message. Generally these marketing efforts showcase the business and the brand, present a compelling value proposition, and strive to make a powerful and lasting impression on the audience.

While these traditional marketing mediums are important, they rarely trump the return on investment of a good business success story or case study. Case studies are effective because they transcend marketing hype and provide a real-world example of how the seller's product or service delivered promised results to a real-world customer.

Most marketing collateral is conceptual and requires a degree of vision and analysis from the audience. Case studies, on the other hand, are practical and tell a story, making them easy to understand and relate to, especially if they are tailored for a specific industry. Case studies get prospects involved by creating an emotional connection between the reader and a problem or challenge they share with other decision makers and organizations, and they lend credibility by providing actual, quantifiable, believable validation of ROI from a tangible organization.

Crafting Case Studies

In the process of measuring initial results and capturing best practices at each implementation, you will document how and where your product or service has improved each client's business and delivered the promised ROI. This is also an opportunity to create new and compelling case studies.

Over time, you can build a library of case studies which become the heart of your marketing mantra in the pursuit of new prospects. I recommend formatting case studies using these elements in this order:

- Get the reader's attention.

- Provide an overview of the client's business.

- Provide a description of the client's current situation, challenges, and problems.

- Offer a description of the solutions provided.

- Summarize the quantifiable results delivered by the solution.

Get the reader's attention by using a headline or customer quotation that flaunts the end results and benefits the customer received by implementing your solutions. The use of startling and quantifiable statistics is very effective. For example, "Our sales increased 37% in the first quarter we implemented this program." Or, "We were able to reduce operating costs an average of 26% per month as a result of implementing the services provided."

Provide an overview of the client's business and business model to help prospects relate to the case study. The overview should include what industry the client is in, the size of the organization, geographic scope, and even industry trends driving change or creating challenges.

Provide a description of the client's current challenges and problems by telling the story of the client's missed opportunities, dysfunctions, high total cost of ownership, or low productivity. Don't hold back here. Be graphic in telling a story which makes the audience *feel the pain* the client was experiencing. Include "before" photographs or charts and customer quotations to add drama.

Offer a description of the solutions provided, now that the audience relates to the client profiled and feels the pain. Briefly describe the product, service, or program implemented to eliminate the pain. Describe your consultative process of analyze–design–implement–manage relative to how your solutions came about and were implemented. Again, use quotations from the customer to proclaim how the implementation of the recommended solutions had a quantifiable positive impact on their business. You can also use "after" photographs or charts to show the improvements and results delivered.

Summarize the quantifiable results delivered by the solution including validated return on investment, reduced total cost of ownership, or increased productivity. Also flaunt the related side effects, including intangible benefits such as improved competitive advantage, customer retention, or employee morale.

Sample Case Studies

Here are some sample marketing case studies that follow the format presented here, three of which are very comprehensive and one of which nets the message in one simple page.

>> FranklinCovey Applications Support Best Shore

eds.com

Customer Profile

www.franklincovey.com

FranklinCovey is the global leader in effectiveness training, productivity tools and assessment services for organizations, teams, and individuals.

Offices: Headquartered in Salt Lake City, Utah, with approximately 100 retail stores

Founded:

1984 - Franklin Day Planner

1989 - Dr. Stephen Covey published The Seven Habits of Highly Effective People; developed training and consulting business

1997 - The two firms merged into FranklinCovey

Industry: Consumer Industries and Retail

Employees: 1,400

Highlights

Goal: Lower operational costs associated with applications support services while maintaining the current levels of support and services for key business applications.

Solutions: EDS implemented a Best Shore support model, allowing the delivery of multi-tiered support from a variety of global locations, and optimizing resources to solve critical business needs and changes in applications software.

Results: FranklinCovey realized a cost savings of 20 percent, or $4.2M over the previous contract costs, while experiencing 99 percent and above performance on critical service levels, including response and resolution time, availability, and service hours.

FranklinCovey Optimizes Applications Support and Reduces Costs Using EDS' Best Shore^{SM} Support Solution

FranklinCovey, with more than $280M in revenue from its core offerings, wanted efficient and effectively managed support of its key business applications. Though pleased with its current applications support contract with EDS, FranklinCovey needed to reduce application support costs and redirect resources to its business units without impairing service. With EDS' Best Shore solution, FranklinCovey optimized its Applications Support Help Desk with operational and cost savings of 20 percent, or $4.2M. FranklinCovey also enjoys higher-skilled resources, more support personnel and shorter issue resolution times, through the Best Shore solution's "follow the sun" approach. Throughout the engagement, EDS reached service levels greater than 99 percent in critical business areas of availability, response and resolution time, and service hours.

The Challenge: Decrease Applications Support Costs While Maintaining Service Levels and Availability; Channel Savings to Other Core Areas

FranklinCovey was in the midst of restructuring its offerings and was examining where to implement savings and best support its new market approach. EDS had been providing applications support services covering key business applications, which supported FranklinCovey's revenue-generating activities for the previous five years. These applications included ERP Software, Tax Engine and EDI Software, Retail Application Software, E-Commerce Platform, Financial Software, CRM products and Internal Project-Sharing Applications.

EDS carefully managed, communicated and implemented all code changes, fixes and patches to have minimal impact on the business.

"The EDS Best Shore model has allowed us to optimize our on-shore and off-shore resource mix, managing our business critical applications through the most efficient model and providing quick responses as our needs change."

Mike Connelly
Vice President of Information Technology
FranklinCovey

Given the challenges of declining revenues in the post-9/11 business environment, FranklinCovey introduced a number of initiatives to reduce selling, general and administrative costs, so they could be better aligned with the company's new business reality. As part of one of those initiatives FranklinCovey challenged its IT partner, EDS, to find a better way to manage these business-critical applications – including ways that might provide an even higher level of service while minimizing the business risk.

What FranklinCovey Wanted

FranklinCovey wanted an IT partner with the expertise to most effectively manage its business applications support needs, while meeting its financial and service level requirements. The key criteria were:

- Reduce outsourcing expenses
- Maintain the skill set and experience of support resources
- Provide additional resources that could support new application implementations and upgrades
- Provide control and flexibility wherever resources are deployed – internal FranklinCovey, and EDS Best Shore

FranklinCovey Chooses EDS

The superior service EDS had provided to FranklinCovey through the Applications Management and Delivery contract over the previous five years provided a baseline for FranklinCovey to evaluate a change to the outsourcing approach. The in-place agreement enabled a team of FranklinCovey and EDS employees to provide the best services from the most logical resources. EDS' Best Shore solution raised this arrangement to a higher level, through greater availability and higher skill levels. It was critical that the vendor chosen be able to work within an environment that was partially in-house and partially outsourced, while still seamlessly providing application support services to the organization.

Chapter Six

The Bottom Line for FranklinCovey

By modifying the contract, the joint team significantly increased the benefits to FranklinCovey. A key component of the success was the joint approach to defining which activities were best suited to be handled on-site, directly by the end user and which could be supported through the Best Shore resources. One major advantage was that application requirements could be gathered during the day in Salt Lake City, and then sent to the developers to work on through the night, with testing ready to be implemented the next day. Change management is a critical component of this process, along with implementing fixes, patches and upgrades. FranklinCovey found the 24-hour clock and structured change management process worked well. Domestic resources provided final code review and managed the entire process to ensure continuity in meeting and exceeding all compliance standards, such as Sarbanes-Oxley.

The team also considered the impact on business continuity and the level of business risk of this decision, thereby ensuring that business interruptions were minimal and transparent to users. FranklinCovey experienced several benefits in service through the process as well – with more staff available to support the applications, access to higher skilled resources, and minimized impact on business continuity.

These key improvements, all met while experiencing significant costs savings, evolved in different ways. Accepting the Best Shore model was easy because of the successful, five-year-old outsourcing model. Before the transition, the team planned extensively, and thoroughly considered the placement of roles based on business risk and continuity. Once the Best Shore model was implemented, 24-hour availability brought huge benefits and increased the continuity of access to the applications. Problem resolution now typically occurs overnight as does the implementation of fixes, patches or new versions of software, minimizing impact on the daily business. With a strong change management process in place, all changes underwent sufficient testing and review, with minimal disruptions to productivity, thanks to the 24-hour schedule.

Finally, the mix of FranklinCovey employees and EDS Best Shore resources actually freed in-house employees to support FranklinCovey's needs. This scalability allowed domestic staff to focus on high business value activity, while much of the support work was done by the increased staff at the Best Shore centers.

With the transition, FranklinCovey has continued to experience high service levels and support coverage, with problem resolution now occurring overnight and without interrupting the business day. In addition, the skill level of the EDS' Best Shore centers is typically a CMMI level 4 or 5 certification, providing FranklinCovey with a highly skilled and knowledgeable support staff for its critical business applications. All this has come with a 20 percent operational savings to FranklinCovey, allowing it to focus on realigning its core business services to offer the best solution to the dynamic, technology-driven market. And the market has responded. Prior to the EDS engagement, customer satisfaction was an impressive 90 percent; today, it's a staggering 98 percent.

FranklinCovey's Bottom Line for the Project:

A 20 percent operational cost savings, representing $4.2M over the remainder of its contract with EDS, and a increased level of responsiveness and support that allows FranklinCovey to focus on its core services and offerings.

"Changing to the EDS Best Shore operating model has had the desired outcome, as IT can now provide 24X7 application support to address the business' needs, while enhancing the IT resources skill set without increasing costs."

Mike Connelly
Vice President of Information Technology
FranklinCovey

112

The Business Case for Case Studies

case study | FranklinCovey Applications Support Best Shore

Benefits

The charts on this page illustrate some of the improvements that FranklinCovey has experienced by partnering with EDS Best Shore for its application support needs.

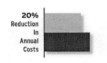

20%
Reduction
In
Annual
Costs

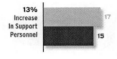

13%
Increase
In Support
Personnel

17

15

Post Best Shore

Pre Best Shore

Current Service Level Performance

Service Category Level	Service Level	Performance Level
Availability	99 percent	99.95 percent
Response Time	30 min	99.95 percent
Resolution Time	8 hr	99.85 percent
Service Hours	24 x 7	99.95 percent

Objective	Benefits Achieved
Reduce outsourcing expenses	FranklinCovey experienced a 20 percent operational cost savings of $4.2M over the remainder of its contract with EDS
Maintain skill set and experience of support resources	With a smooth transition ensuring that all onshore knowledge moved to EDS Best Shore centers, there was no degradation in skill sets, and the CMMI certification levels of the support staff increased
Provide additional resources that could support new application implementations and upgrades	Based on the allocation of outsourced resources, additional staff provided FranklinCovey with more support and a "sun never sets" environment for applications development and testing

EDS. Technology services. Business solutions.
We help clients improve their systems and processes so they can become more productive, manage change and grow.

Contact
EDS
5400 Legacy Drive
Plano, Texas 75024-3199
phone: 1 800 566 9337
visit: eds.com
e-mail: info@eds.com

FranklinCovey Looks to the Future

The partnership established between FranklinCovey and EDS has grown stronger through the implementation of this Best Shore solution. Service levels were always high, even under the earlier outsourcing model. Today, the availability of resources and the ability to respond to new requests and development needs overnight has increased satisfaction, providing benchmark levels of business continuity. With sound operational guidelines monitoring the development and implementation of critical changes and updates to FranklinCovey's core business applications, FranklinCovey can remain focused on its business services. As FranklinCovey continues to evolve its approach to its market, it looks to EDS to continue providing it with high levels of flexibility and service.

mainstay partners
making technology investments count

BUSINESS BENEFITS SERIES

BUSINESS BENEFITS SERIES HIGHLIGHTS

- Investment payback in 12 months
- Fast online submission and approval of T&E expenses
- 118% increase in staff productivity, enabling consolidation of T&E processing centers
- 51% decrease in cost of processing T&E reports
- More accurate categorization of expenses, leading to increase in tax deductions
- Detailed monitoring of card usage patterns, reducing business risk
- Comprehensive information supplied to management, improving decision making ability
- Reduced system integration costs; no need for additional hardware

COMPANY PROFILE

MasterCard International

Purchase, New York
www.mastercard.com

MasterCard International is a leading global payments solutions company that provides a broad variety of innovative services in support of global members' credit, deposit access, electronic cash, business-to-business and related payment programs.

Industry
Financial Services

President and Chief Executive Officer
Robert W. Selander

MasterCard's New T&E Expense System Boosts Productivity 118%; Cuts Reporting Costs 51%, Projects Savings of $2.8 Million

EXECUTIVE SUMMARY

It's not surprising that MasterCard International excels at the art of transaction processing. One of most recognized brands for global payments, MasterCard performs more than one trillion transactions each year for a full range of payment programs and services.

Yet when it came to processing the company's own travel and entertainment (T&E) transactions, MasterCard saw room for improvement. Like many organizations, it had a manually intensive T&E system based on spreadsheets and paper receipts. As a result, coordinators at the company's T&E processing centers spent an inordinate amount of time re-entering data to fix submission errors.

With its extensive transaction-processing experience, MasterCard knew it could improve the process by combining an online T&E expense management solution with the MasterCard Corporate Card, thus ensuring greater productivity and efficiency. In addition, the company saw an opportunity to better enforce compliance by using an electronic process that seamlessly integrated card transaction data within the expense report.

In 2003, MasterCard deployed Oracle Internet Expenses, an Oracle E-Business Suite application for T&E reporting and approval. The online application works in tandem with the MasterCard payment system to quickly validate and approve expense reports while flagging unusual transactions for further investigation.

According to study by independent consultant Mainstay Partners, MasterCard has seen a range of efficiency gains since implementing the system, including a 118% rise in labor productivity at its processing centers, a 51% reduction in T&E reporting costs, and 43% fewer IT issues related to the reports. The company has also captured more tax deductions from the system's ability to categorize expenses automatically.

Efficiencies generated by the system enabled MasterCard to consolidate two distinct T&E processing centers into one, and managers said it is helping transform the T&E organization into a more proactive, information-driven team. Assuming current trends continue, Mainstay estimates that the combined MasterCard-Oracle expense management system could generate as much as $2.8 million in net benefits over five years when compared to MasterCard's previous T&E expense management system.

ORACLE
PRODUCTS AND SERVICES

- Oracle Financials
- Oracle Internet Expenses
- Oracle Human Resources

> "We looked at multiple vendors, but with Oracle we got out-of-the-box functionality. In keeping with the 80/20 rule— anytime you can avoid integration, you have to go with it."
>
> **Tim Westendorf**
> Vice President
> Financial Systems
> MasterCard International

PROJECT BACKGROUND

MasterCard began focusing on ways to improve its T&E system in 2003. At that time, most employees filled out expense reports by keying transactions into a spreadsheet. Besides being time intensive, the manual reporting was error prone, making it hard for workers at the company's two T&E processing centers to keep up with an expanding workload. "We realized it no longer made any sense to continue processing expenses manually when there was a faster, less expensive, more accurate alternative," said Lillian Tropea, vice president, accounting, MasterCard International.

MasterCard officials said they selected Oracle's T&E application—Oracle Internet Expenses—because it was a "mature solution from a mature company." Another selling point was the tight integration between the T&E application and MasterCard's financial and accounting solution (Oracle Financials). "We looked at multiple vendors, but with Oracle we got out-of-the-box functionality. In keeping with the 80/20 rule [Pareto's principle of time management], anytime you can avoid integration, you have to go with it," said Tim Westendorf, vice president of financial systems for MasterCard International. Plus the company could use existing hardware and manage the solution with its current IT staff.

MasterCard moved quickly once the selection was made, taking only 120 days to complete a global rollout, including a brief test period. The company attributes an internal training program held on site, along with Web casts for remote employees, for rapid and widespread acceptance of the application.

INCREASED PRODUCTIVITY

With MasterCard's new expense-management system, Tropea explained, "employees no longer have to key T&E transactions into a spreadsheet or wait until the end of the month to process expense reports." Instead, cardholding employees log into Oracle Internet Expenses and call up their credit card transaction data, which is sent electronically by the card-issuing bank daily. With just a mouse click, cardholders populate new expense reports directly with the card transaction data, which saves time and ensures that expenses are correctly categorized for tax reporting purposes.

Next, the system's built-in workflow function routes the expense reports to managers for approval and then on to MasterCard's T&E processing center. Because the reports are more accurate, the processing staff spends far less time reconciling and reentering data. As illustrated in Figure 1, MasterCard's T&E staff productivity has risen 118%, with each full-time T&E team member now processing up to 600 T&E reports per month, compared to 300 before the Oracle implementation.

2

" With Oracle Internet
Expenses, employees no
longer have to key T&E
transactions into a
spreadsheet or wait until
the end of the month to
process expense
reports. "

Lillian Tropea
Vice President
Accounting
MasterCard International

FIGURE 1: PRODUCTIVITY IMPROVED 118%

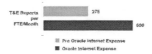

T&E Reports per FTE/Month — 275 (Pre Oracle Internet Expense), 600 (Oracle Internet Expense)

▒ Pre Oracle Internet Expense
▓ Oracle Internet Expense

The Mainstay study noted a 51% reduction in the cost of processing each expense report—from $19.50 to $9.50 (See Figure 2). In addition, the efficiency boost has allowed MasterCard to consolidate its two T&E processing centers, with a headcount savings of two T&E coordinators and 0.5 managers. "Now the T&E team is empowered to 'think' and provide more value to the organization," Tropea said, "and not just focus on moving stacks and stacks of paper."

FIGURE 2: COST OF PROCESSING T&E REPORT REDUCED BY 51%

Cost to Process a T&E Report — $19.50 (Pre Oracle Internet Expense), $9.50 (Oracle Internet Expense)

▒ Pre Oracle Internet Expense
▓ Oracle Internet Expense

The study found that the integration of Oracle Internet Expenses with MasterCard's existing Oracle Financials application simplified system security and management, largely because there are fewer systems and interfaces to maintain. It also simplifies the software upgrade path and makes it easier to scale the system as business needs grow.

As Figure 3 illustrates, the consolidated footprint has reduced IT support demands significantly. Following a slight adjustment period, the number of monthly support issues related to T&E reporting dropped 43.5%, from 313 to 177 each month.

> " Now the T&E team is empowered to 'think' and add value to the organization and not just focused on moving stacks and stacks of paper. "
>
> Lillian Tropea
> Vice President
> Accounting
> MasterCard International

FIGURE 3: T&E REPORTING ISSUES LOWERED BY 43.5%

Number of IT Issues Related to T&E Expense Reporting per Month: 313 / 177

▨ Pre Oracle Internet Expense
▨ Oracle Internet Expense

LOWER RISK, BOOST IN TAX DEDUCTIONS

With the Oracle solution, MasterCard deals quickly with inactive accounts because its processing center analyzes statements from card-issuing banks on a daily basis. Consequently, MasterCard identifies and cancels inactive or dormant accounts quickly, reducing overall corporate liability. Mainstay noted a 300% improvement in managing card cancellations, as illustrated in Figure 4. Compared to the previous system, in which only 100 cards were cancelled each year, today the team is identifying idle or errant accounts—and canceling the associated cards—at a rate of about 400 per year.

The increase in cancellations is a significant safeguard because at any given time MasterCard International has approximately 2,500 corporate cards in use. MasterCard's T&E team can identify and act on questionable transactions almost immediately, reducing potential losses due to fraud. MasterCard also monitors credit and cash advance limits to further reduce risk.

FIGURE 4: 300% IMPROVEMENT MANAGING CREDIT CARD CANCELLATIONS

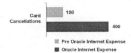

Card Cancellations: 100 / 400

▨ Pre Oracle Internet Expense
▨ Oracle Internet Expense

Mainstay found that Oracle Internet Expenses, when combined with MasterCard's payment solution, contributed significantly to improving MasterCard's tax advantage. Today, MasterCard uses the system to automatically assign expenses to the appropriate tax account, saving time and enabling MasterCard to book substantially more tax deductions than before. In fact, since the deployment, MasterCard has reduced the amount of lost tax deductions by 900%, translating into approximately $600,000 in annual net benefits from improved tax savings and reduced professional fees for outside audits.

4

> " We are amazed at the enormous impact the combination of MasterCard products, in concert with Oracle Financials and Internet Expenses has had on our business. "
>
> **Stephen W. Orfei**
> Senior Vice President,
> Advanced Payments
> MasterCard International

FIGURE 5: CAPTURING AVAILABLE TAX DEDUCTIONS IMPROVES 900%

Estimated Lost Tax Deductions — $1,300,00 / $130,000

■ Pre Oracle Internet Expense
■ Oracle Internet Expense

THE POWER OF INFORMATION

From a strategic perspective, Mainstay concluded that the deployment has allowed MasterCard to generate more value from its spending information. By analyzing the wealth of time-and-expense data in the system, the company can provide crucial intelligence to senior management and improve decisionmaking.

"Intuitively we felt that using Oracle Internet Expenses with the MasterCard suite of products would generate value," said Stephen W. Orfei, senior vice president, advanced payments at MasterCard. "We are amazed at the enormous impact the combination of MasterCard products, in concert with Oracle Financials and Internet Expenses has had on our business."

BENEFITS SUMMARY

Assuming current trends continue, Mainstay estimated that the combined MasterCard-Oracle expense management system has the potential for generating as much as $2.8 million in net benefits over five years when compared to MasterCard's previous T&E system.

Table 1 summarizes the costs and benefits of the Oracle deployment projected over five years. The total five-year investment of about $600,000 includes the costs of Oracle licenses, annual maintenance, consulting, and internal labor. Total benefits of $3.4 million include labor productivity and tax savings projected over five years[1].

Figure 6 shows Mainstay's cost and benefit projections year-by-year over the investment period[1]. According to the study, MasterCard's investment paid for itself about 12 months after the system was deployed.

---

[1] Projections assume continuation of current trends. Actual results may vary.

5

mainstay partners
making technology investments count

BUSINESS BENEFITS SERIES

ABOUT THE BUSINESS BENEFITS SERIES

This study is one of a series of investigations into the costs and business returns of IT investments, with a focus on Oracle technology and applications. It is intended to serve business executives and managers who are evaluating technology investment options.

Research and analysis for this study was conducted by Mainstay Partners, an independent consulting firm, and was based on interviews with executives at MasterCard International, review of company planning documents, and searches of industry literature. ROI calculations use industry standard assumptions regarding the time value of money.

Information contained in the publication has been obtained from sources considered reliable, but is not warranted by Mainstay Partners. Copyright © 2005 Oracle.

ORACLE

Published June 2005

Table 1
Estimated Costs and Benefits Over Five Years

COSTS	
Oracle Licenses[2]	$150,000
Annual Maintenance	$140,000
Consulting Costs	$150,000
Internal Labor[3]	$158,393
Total 5 Year Investment	$598,393
BENEFITS	
Headcount Savings	$1,016,000
Other Quantifiable Savings[4]	$2,400,000
Total Benefits	$3,416,000
TOTAL 5 YEAR NET BENEFITS	$2,817,607

1. Costs and benefits are estimates only; actual results may vary.
2. Oracle Internet Expense less rebate for previous software of $30,000. No additional hardware required or retired.
3. Includes IFS, GTO, business analyst and training costs.
4. Includes increase in documented claimable business expenses deductions, and the current costs of research etc. resulting in approximately $600,000 per year in savings.

Source: Mainstay Partners/MasterCard

FIGURE 6: FIVE-YEAR ESTIMATED RETURNS

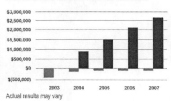

Actual results may vary

For more information about MasterCard ExpenSys on the Oracle platform, please send an email to eB2B@mastercard.com.

Chapter Six

seadoo guru
interactive kiosk

BRP

THE RELATIONSHIP AGENCY™

CASE STUDY

SEA·DOO GURU

CLIENT OVERVIEW

bombardier recreational products

Bombardier Recreational Products (BRP), a division of Bombardier Inc., is a leading manufacturer of Personal Water Craft (PWC) based in Montreal, Quebec, Canada. Bombardier Recreational Products manufactures Sea-Doo™ watercraft and Sport Boats, the premier PWCs by which all other manufacturers are measured.

SITUATION

BRP sought to inform current and prospective PWC users about innovative technological advancements, environmental breakthroughs, and boating safety guidelines at industry shows and dealer venues where boaters would be in attendance. Bombardier hoped to reach the market in an inventive, interactive way. In addition, Bombardier needed an unobtrusive means of capturing user information for market research and future marketing initiatives.

Chapter Six

SOLUTION

MindComet concepted and created the Sea-Doo Guru, an interactive, touch screen kiosk that incorporates entertainment, information, and technology into an educational platform. To attract customers and dealers at industry shows, the kiosk was constructed out of a real Sea-Doo PWC body and hull standing upright for maximum visual impact. At the base of this structure are blue, cartoon-like waves, making the Sea-Doo appear as if it is leaping out of the water. The interactive touch screen and keyboard are placed approximately where the handlebars should be, giving the user the impression that they are "behind the wheel" of a personal watercraft.

Conceptual Drawing

Despite its striking external appearance, the bulk of this project was on the inside. The hardware, a powerful, Pentium® 4 based PC, allows users to easily maneuver through five entertaining modules via the plasma touch screen. The five games are designed to educate users, while at the same time gathering valuable demographic information.

MEETING KEY OBJECTIVES

During industry shows, companies vie for attendee attention in ever more creative and innovative ways. Generally speaking, the more extravagant and visually appealing a display, the more visitors are likely to stop and spend time at these booths. Bombardier wanted something to differentiate them from hundreds of standard displays. The question was "How?"

The concept of an experiential learning kiosk allows Bombardier to enhance consumers' knowledge while at the same time establishing Bombardier

as a progressive, environmentally conscious, and technologically advanced manufacturer of personal watercraft. The informative and innovative game modules educate PWC users while gathering demographic information. The Sea-Doo Guru, with its extraordinary visual presence and interactive functionality, made a remarkable debut at the Montreal Boat Show in March 2002.

Completed Sea·Doo Guru

3

SEA·DOO GURU

*"The Sea-Doo Guru
represents an entirely
new way to connect to
and educate the public."*

· Fernando Garcia
Director of Public &
Regulatory Affairs
Bombardier Recreational
Products

MEETING KEY OBJECTIVES

During industry shows, companies vie for attendee attention in ever more
creative and innovative ways. Generally speaking, the more extravagant and
visually appealing a display, the more visitors are likely to stop and spend
time at these booths. Bombardier wanted something to differentiate them
from hundreds of standard displays. The question was "How?"

The concept of an experiential learning kiosk allows Bombardier to enhance
consumers' knowledge while at the same time establishing Bombardier as
a progressive, environmentally conscious, and technologically advanced
manufacturer of personal watercraft. The informative and innovative game
modules educate PWC users while gathering demographic information. The
Sea-Doo Guru, with its extraordinary visual presence and interactive functionality,
made a remarkable debut at the Montreal Boat Show in March 2002.

DIRECT RESULTS

captured the attention of passers-by

The Sea-Doo Guru's phenomenal debut in Montreal left Bombardier
representatives extremely satisfied with the increase of visitors drawn to their
booth. They attribute the increase entirely to the addition of the Sea-Doo
Guru to their display. The Guru, which is bright yellow and stands nearly 7 feet
tall, can be seen from a distance, providing the Bombardier representatives
with an unusual competitive advantage over their trade show neighbors;

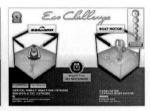

they were the only manufacturers with a vertical, computerized personal watercraft.

Trade show representatives reported that the Guru was their single-most successful display piece ever, not only because the attendees were so impressed, but also because the Guru, with its informative modules, explained many aspects of the Sea-Doo, thereby freeing their time to attract more people to the booth.

gathered information for ongoing marketing activities

As the user works through the five-part course toward the goal of completing all modules, a full demographic profile is stored on the computer. This profile can be used for future direct marketing campaigns and aggregated for demographic and marketing research.

established sea-doo as an industry leader

Four of the five software modules are dedicated to safety and the environment. The heavy emphasis on boater responsibility and pollutant reduction through experiential learning was a core objective of the Guru project. Sea-Doo has always been a leading industry promoter of responsible boating, yet getting that information out to consumers in a creative way was a persistent challenge before the Guru. The final module presents an "Innovation Showcase", a self-promotional tool that outlines Bombardier's latest personal watercraft technologies, establishing the company as a leader in technological advancement.

5

about**mindcomet**

MindComet assists clients in optimizing their customer relationships. We work cooperatively to develop a comprehensive customer relationship strategy that strengthens the bond to both existing customers and prospects. Our strategy integrates and automates diverse input from a company's internal and external sales, marketing, advertising, customer service and public relations to create detailed, individualized customer dialogues that build brand equity, increase customer conversion rates, decrease acquisition costs and extend the lifetime value of each relationship.

ORLANDO · NEW YORK · ATLANTA · LOS ANGELES

www.mindcomet.com · sales@mindcomet.com
1.800.668.1761x2

Workforce Solutions

Brewing a high-quality workforce for the busy season at Starbucks

Supplementing Production

Business Issue:

Starbucks Coffee Company's roasting plant in Kent, Washington ships thousands of pounds of coffee each day during the holiday season. To handle the increase in consumer demand from its retail, catalog and online outlets during peak season, Starbucks needs hundreds of supplemental production, packaging and distribution workers. Realizing the importance of having a qualified, supplemental workforce, Starbucks sought a staffing supplier with a proven testing process for assessing a range of industrial skills.

Manpower Solution:

Starbucks chose Manpower as its primary supplier of supplemental staff because of its validated set of industrial skills assessments -- Ultradex®. This assessment effectively identifies applicants with the skills and aptitude needed to work productively in production and distribution environments.

Initially, Manpower created skill profiles associated with the various jobs at the roasting plant by administering Ultradex to some of Starbucks' most productive plant workers. This process established benchmark scores, which Manpower uses to select workers who meet or exceed Starbucks' skill requirements. Different combinations of Ultradex tests are used to select the best people for different areas of the plant.

To manage the company's supplemental workforce year-round, Manpower placed an on-site coordinator at the roasting plant. Additionally, Manpower developed a strategic recruiting plan to meet the high volume of people needed to support Starbucks' peak season.

Benefits:

For several years, Manpower has helped Starbucks get its product to market on time during the holiday season. During the first peak season in which Manpower used Ultradex at the company, Starbucks' error rate for products shipped declined 40 percent. Retention of supplemental staff during peak season has increased significantly through the years, which maximizes Starbucks' investment in training supplemental workers in proper packaging techniques. Manpower's relationship with Starbucks has expanded to include placement of supplemental administrative staff at Starbucks corporate offices in downtown Seattle as well.

"Over time, manpower and Starbucks have developed a strong relationship that has been significant in supporting the growth of our business and our ability to deliver high-quality products to our customers," said the vice president, human resources, Starbucks Supply Chain Operations.

Manpower

Leveraging Case Studies to Create Selling Opportunities

Once you have developed a repertoire of case studies, your entire sales force can incorporate them into the prospecting phase of the sales process. Case studies are hugely effective when presented in marketing collateral, sales letters, and tele-marketing approaches to secure initial sales appointments with new prospects.

On initial sales appointments many sellers bore the prospect with the typical "We're really big, we've been in business a long time, and look at these pictures of all of our employees in front of the fancy corporate headquarters" presentation. Worse, they follow up with the always boring, "Here is a brochure describing our newest product or service."

What decision makers really want to know in the first ten minutes is: What can your organization, products, and services do to improve my business, help me meet my objectives, address my challenges, reduce my total cost of ownership, improve productivity, or gain a competitive advantage?

At a first meeting, executives are wondering if sellers are expert professionals or empty-suit wannabes. They want to know if you have actually delivered results to clients in their industry, in similar size companies and in similar operating environments. They want to know about your engagement process and how you go about doing what you say you can do.

The presentation of a case study provides you with the perfect opportunity to fully explain the consultative engagement process of analyze, design, implement, and manage. Case studies from industry-specific references go a long way in establishing your credibility as an expert resource with a sound process and a product or service offering that delivers results in a similar environment. No advertising campaign, corporate brochure, or showroom does more to articulate how the prospect will benefit by engaging you.

We're almost finished. Let's take a look at the last phase of this process: becoming a true partner for your best clients and creating relationships that stand the test of time, protecting you from competitive threats and expanding your future sales opportunities.

PART THREE

Achieving Partner Status

From Collaboration to Partnering: Moving Towards Partner Status

When implemented properly, the pure play consultative process creates the opportunity to transcend the traditional vendor status and become a respected partner.

Most every company depends on its vendors to help increase efficiency, streamline operations, reduce costs, and deliver their products and services faster. Thus collaboration and the building of strong relationships are key to adhering to budgets and meeting deadlines and quality expectations on a consistent basis.

Many buyers and sellers develop *good relationships*, trust, and even like each other and operate from a "Let's work together and hope for the best" perspective. In this section I suggest that if sellers are to go beyond the status of vendor to become true partners, they need to go well beyond good intentions and commit to a formal partnering process.

The Partnering Process

On this subject I rely on the contribution of my friend and colleague Jim Eisenhart, a partnering specialist and founder of Ventura Consulting Group. According to Jim, partnering with clients means entering the relationship with the *state of mind* of intentionally creating an optimal working relationship. According to Jim the three key components of the formal partnering process are:

1. Setting explicit, challenging, and measurable common goals.

2. Establishing a collaborative process to support the achievement of these goals.

3. Developing a systematic process for resolving issues.

In setting explicit and challenging goals, both partners need to collaborate and set goals that can only be accomplished through the partnership—not by each party acting alone. The establishment of extraordinary goals calls for extraordinary performance from each partner and cannot be achieved with a business-as-usual approach. Partnering creates an opportunity to recognize the unique strengths of each partner and work together to harness these strengths to achieve common goals.

Some examples of explicit and challenging coals include:

■ Increasing sales by 35% within the next six months.

■ Achieving a 100% customer satisfaction rating.

■ Delivering 100% uptime.

■ Bringing a construction project in eight months ahead of schedule and 20% under budget.

Beyond being explicit and challenging, goals should have measurable benchmarks and a defined joint monitoring process. Partners need to devote face time on a predetermined schedule to review progress and make any adjustments to implementation that are needed to achieve the goals.

In this collaborative process, partners work together to develop an action plan that supports the achievement of their mutual goals. The action plan includes:

■ *What* methods, resources, and tools will be deployed.

■ *Who* will be responsible for the deployment.

■ *When* this deployment will occur.

Eisenhart advises clients to be "ruthlessly specific" here and to sweat the small stuff. This means both partners need to articulate specific requests of one another, offer proposals and counterproposals, and arrive at a joint agreement to execute their roles with 100% commitment.

This *who does what when* collaboration goes a long way in preparing the way for a smooth implementation of the products being placed or services being rendered. This planning also sets the foundation for the management phase in the pure play consulting process.

Bumps in the Road

Even in good relationships and partnerships, things can and will go wrong. Issues and problems can create speed bumps or outright breakdowns in implementation and challenge the achievement of the goals. But many issues and problems are predictable, and some proactive planning can prevent them or at least mitigate their impact on implementation and on the partner relationship.

The first step in developing a systematic process to resolve issues is to predict what problems will probably be encountered beforehand. Both partners need to think through and articulate the problems they encountered during past experiences implementing similar projects. Partners must also identify the most complex stages of implementation and predict the potential problems that are most likely to crop up.

According to Eisenhart, a key approach in resolving issues is for both partners to agree that any issue will be resolved as a team without casting blame. Instead the emphasis will always be on working together towards a solution.

When an issue or problem creates a speed bump or break-down, partners need to collaborate on an action plan to resolve it. This means going back to the *who does what when* drill. Partners need to brainstorm all methods, resources, tools, and options which could be deployed to solve the problem and then make a clear action plan with completion dates and a commitment to execute.

As a practical matter, through partnering the buyer saves tremendous time and effort evaluating potential vendors, soliciting proposals, viewing sales presentations, and negotiating and managing contracts from multiple vendors. By consolidating these and other activities related to managing the vendors with a sole partner, the buyer can leverage purchasing power, increase partner accountability, and streamline procurement administration processes—all saving time and money.

In the 1970s Xerox embarked on a partnering initiative and went from 10,000 *vendors* to 3,000 *partners*. Motorola implemented a partnering initiative and went from 9,000 *vendors* to 3,000 *partners*. The buyer who practices partnering benefits in the long run from *getting things right* versus *getting things cheaper*.

Keys to Successful Partnerships

While there are scores of books dedicated to the art and science of partnering, I will offer here some best practices or keys to successful partnerships based on my personal experience and that of my clients.

Top-Management Sponsorship

Top management from both partners needs to convey the vision for, commitment to, and importance of the partnership to mid-level management, who are the chief stakeholders and implementers. The mantra "Managers focus on what their managers focus on" is the foundation to getting started on the right foot.

Top management must provide mid-level managers with clear responsibility, authority, and initiative to marshal internal resources to get the job done.

Multiple Relationships at Multiple Levels

Top management must also have relationships with their counterparts at the partner's organization.

All stakeholders and implementers must have direct access to people who can help overcome challenges, respond to requests, and successfully complete tasks.

All implementers must have good relationships within their own organization and credibility among their peers.

Interpersonal relationships require face time. This results in mutual respect as team members work toward a common goal, and breeds patience and a willingness to work through problems instead of placing blame. In the process of working together, both parties develop a respect for each other's expertise, skills, and knowledge.

Communication and Timely Access to Information

Communication builds trust. It is essential that connections between implementers are streamlined. Implementers need to be able to pick up the phone and talk to each other versus going through a cumbersome chain of command.

Implementers need to share internal processes and be candid about internal political and personal issues. As each partner communicates why things are the way they are within their organization, each can better accept and adapt to situations.

Each partner must listen to, acknowledge, and consider each other's requests, proposals, and counterproposals with the intention of arriving at a win/win agreement.

Feedback is important in any relationship. Formal project management and account reviews among management are essential. Feedback between implementers on an ongoing basis must be constant.

Flexibility

Each partner must be willing to adapt its business processes, procedures, protocols, and even operating models to accommodate each other's requirements. This includes, at a minimum, streamlining transaction processes, purchase authorizations, invoice processing, and shipping and receiving protocols.

Do You Have What It Takes to Partner?

Partnering is not for the faint of heart, or those who want to sit back and conduct business as usual. It is not for those who simply deliver lip service or talk a good game while closing a sale, then disappear. Partnering is both an attitude and a discipline that requires diligence, honesty, and full commitment. The return on investment for both partners includes the likelihood of achieving challenging goals and avoiding or reducing the impact of problems encountered along the way.

Let's face it. Sales is hard work, and the implementation of key projects can be stressful. Partnering offers you a less stressful work environment and creates a sense of belonging to a team with pride in what it does and how it goes about doing it. Properly executed, partnering provides participants job security by building a reputation for achieving even the most challenging goals.

Why the Leaders Are the Leaders

Ben & Jerry's, Starbucks, Magnatag, Virgin Atlantic Airlines, Apple Computer, Ritz Carlton, and some cheesy strip club in Amsterdam all sell commodities in mature markets. They all have big-time competition that sell on price, price, price. They all operate in the same economic conditions. Yet all of these market leaders (and thousands of other businesses with names you've never heard) have transcended commodity status and become the premium provider of premium-priced products and services, resulting in vastly increased profits. All have achieved partnership status with their customers, often creating cult-like followings that last for years.

Ten things these organizations have in common:

1. They've made a total commitment to providing outrageous value, from the CEO to the sales clerk to the truck driver.

2. Their business model is built around delivering on that commitment.

3. They focus on value- and premium-centric buyers who recognize and appreciate value and innovation.

4. They have an intimate understanding of their customer's preferences, applications, and issues.

5. They innovate versus emulate. They don't do things the way they are commonly done in their industry. They bring fresh ideas and solutions.

6. They add outrageous value in their consultative sales process that becomes part of a remarkable customer experience.

7. They capture best practices, document successes, and leverage them to develop new customers.

8. They transcend vendor status by partnering with customers, assuring repeat business.

9. They are outrageous themselves. These organizations are full of out-of-the-box thinkers who come up with outrageous ideas like providing passengers a professional masseuse 35,000 feet in the air!

10. They are the most expensive and damn proud of it! They know and proclaim their value proposition relentlessly.

My final appeal to you is this: Ask yourself, whoever you are — CEO, head of marketing, sales manager, salesperson, or delivery driver — "What can I do to add value and deliver a remarkable customer experience worthy of increasing the average transaction value to the equivalent of the $50 ice cream cone?"

That's the scoop on melt-proof profitability. No exotic dancer required.